Macclesfield College

Learning
Resource Centre

k is due fo turn on or before the last d
bel

THE TOTAL CAT MANUAL

David Meyer, Abbie Moore, and Dr. Pia Salk

weldonowen

CONTENTS

Introduction from *Adopt-a-Pet.com*
About *Adopt-a-Pet.com*

 BASICS

☀ BEHAVIOR

HEALTH

CARE

INTRODUCTION

Welcome to the wonderful world of cats. If you have never really known a cat, you are in for an amazing journey! If you have cats, you will find tips and insights here that will help you have a great life with your feline friends.

Cats and humans have been living together since ancient times. Much like dogs, cats have entertained us, given us companionship, and even at times worked for us (keeping rodents out of our homes). Some people say cats are social, and others say they are solitary. Some say they are highly engaged and playful like dogs, and others say they are aloof. Some say they are brave predators, and others say they are shy and quick to run away. Like so many things with cats, all these can be true, given the situation. Cats are affectionate, social, independent, playful, curious, smart, clever, and loving. They are mysterious to those who do not understand them, and wondrous family members and best friends to those who do.

Whether you have one cat in your home or many, we have worked hard to give you all the information you need to understand your cat's behavior and needs. With the tips in this book, you will learn why cats do what they do, what they need to remain happy and healthy, and how to have a wonderful and fulfilling relationship with your own cat. Once you have really known a cat, you will forever be a cat lover. This is the magic power of the feline—let them into your world and you will enter their world—and an amazingly fun world it is! So sit back and enjoy.

Wishing you perches, pounces, and mostly purrs,

David, Abbie, and Pia

David   Abbie   Pia

ABOUT
ADOPT-A-PET.COM

Adopt-a-Pet.com is the world's largest non-profit homeless pet adoption website. Thousands of animal shelters, humane societies, SPCAs, and animal rescue groups post hundreds of thousands of pets for adoption, and millions of potential adopters use adopt-a-pet.com each month to search for pets to adopt. Our service is entirely free, and is made possible by the passionate pet lovers at Nestlé Purina PetCare Company, the Petco Foundation, and Bayer Animal Health.

Our mission is to ensure that every companion animal has a safe and loving home. This means that

1 every pet that is born has a loving home,

2 the human/animal bond is strong and people have all the knowledge and resources they need to have a happy life with their pets, and

3 when a situation arises where a pet really does need a new home, a new and loving home is found.

Our prime tool to help animals is technology. We use the internet to get homeless pets seen and adopted, and to deliver information that allows people to have happy and successful relationships with their pets. We also support animal shelters and companion animal protection organizations of all types by providing technology to help them work faster and smarter.

Technology, however, is not the only tool we use to help companion animals. We also conduct real-world events and publicity campaigns, such as our annual "Pooch Smooch" around Valentines Day, to raise awareness of companion animal issues. Additionally, we conduct campaigns in various cities, featuring local sports stars championing our cause. Those campaigns involve media events, printed billboards, and local radio and TV.

Our team is made up of a small dedicated group of animal lovers, who themselves are often volunteers for local animal shelters and pet-rescue organizations, fostering pets in their homes and helping with weekend adoption events. Our staff played a key role in rescuing many thousands of animals who were stranded in New Orleans in the aftermath of Hurricane Katrina, and are often involved in important issues when we see a way to help animals.

Please visit Adopt-a-Pet.com to learn more and find a pet to adopt near you today.

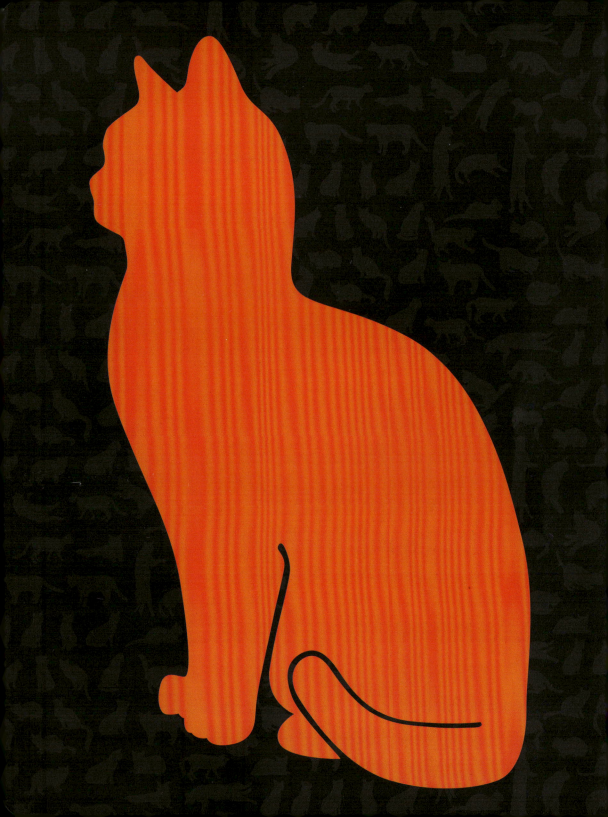

BASICS

> "The smallest feline is a masterpiece."
>
> LEONARDO DA VINCI

So you're thinking of getting a cat—or another cat! There are certain things you should know about bringing a cat into your home and starting a great life with your new companion.

You will need to provide for her physical needs, including shelter, water, food, and medical care, and her psychological needs, such as stimulation, companionship, and love. It's also important that you get to know your cat as an individual—what she likes and doesn't like. When you make human friends, it takes time for them to become comfortable around you. It's the same with your cat; she will blossom and start to reveal her character once she becomes more relaxed in your home. Be gentle and thoughtful. Make the effort to meet her on her own terms and you will discover a deep and fulfilling relationship.

Before you become a pet parent, be sure you are ready for the life long commitment (and joy) of having a cat. Spend time in the planning and you will enjoy your new family member all the more. You will also minimize the chances of any unforeseen challenges as you and your cat get acquainted, and if any problems do arise, you will be well equipped to deal with them.

001 ENJOY THE BENEFITS OF BEING A PET PARENT

Having cats or kittens in your home is not only fun, but can bring certain health benefits as well. Studies show that children as young as nine months old who grow up in homes with cats and dogs are less likely to have issues with allergies and asthma. Playtime with pets has been found to lower blood pressure, and, overall, it can reduce stress, anxiety, and feelings of sadness. You can see why statistics show that people who have pets require fewer doctor's visits. Having a cat can be a calming experience that brings joy and a sense of well-being.

COMPANY One of the nice things about most cats is that if they're not snoozing in the sunlight by the window, they love being around people—even snuggled up in your lap. It is true that some cats can be a bit shy, but generally, once a cat knows you, she becomes much more engaged. Cats can be loyal and friendly, and they are a source of constant entertainment (just ask any cat lover). Many cats will greet you at the door when you come home, and then want nothing more than to be by your side.

And it works both ways—cats are well-liked animals, despite their reputation for sometimes being aloof. Some cities have kitty cafés, where people have the opportunity to be among cat when they're out dining. (Of course, pet parents love these places, too!) Librarians and the owners of bookstores and other shops note how patrons' loyalty increases when they know a kitty or two will greet them when they show up at the door. In some cities, "bodega cats" are common—and some even make it onto the local news.

COMFORT Have you ever noticed that no matter how badly your day is going, when you see a curled-up cat, you start to relax? Cats are remarkably good "nurses" who seem to know when we might benefit from their sweet, unobtrusive presence. Stories abound about the therapeutic effects of cats on nursing home residents and people with Alzheimer's disease, cancer, autism, bipolar disorder, and those struggling with addiction. Cats are also a great source of comfort for people who are grappling with loss or heartbreak. As physician and philosopher Albert Schweitzer once noted, "There are two means of refuge from the miseries of life: music and cats."

002 MEET KITTY— YOUR NEW BOSS

Thousands of years ago, a small, elegant animal began captivating the attention of curious humans. Originally sought out to help with rodent control, the domestic cat, whose scientific name is *Felis catus*, wound up winning over hearts, minds, and laps. Eventually, cats stopped always having to hunt for their supper and they became beloved members of the household. In fact, in ancient Egypt, cats were revered as living deities. And, if the popularity of online cat videos and the sales of kitty-themed apparel, decorations, and any number of other household items are an indication, it's safe to say that they often still are.

003 TEACH KIDS CARE BASICS

Adopting a companion animal who needs a home can help teach important values to children. The decision to devote resources and care to an animal in need is a wonderful statement about a family's underlying values. A child learns about the power of saving a life and about the process of caring for an animal that relies on him. In addition to the many other rewards pet parenting brings, it can give a child a very real sense of how they can have a positive impact in the world.

Spend some time talking to your children about cats and describe the good things they might gain from having a cat in the family: companionship, a playmate, someone to snuggle up to. Also discuss the responsibilities that are involved, such as daily feeding and keeping the litter box clean. Most kids are very keen on the idea of pets, and they will learn so much from having a cat around the home.

FACT OR FICTION?

CATS STEAL BABIES' BREATH

Among the oddest of superstitions is the idea that cats lie on top of babies and steal their breath away. Cats are snuggly by nature and love to curl up with people of all ages, but they are not a threat to sleeping infants. That said, a baby lacks the coordination to move away from a cat who may wish to snuggle near his face or he could poke at the cat, eliciting a swipe of the claw in response. It's wise to keep your kitty out of the cradle.

004 GET THE TIMING RIGHT

Now that you've begun to really map out how you'll accommodate a new kitten or cat, take a moment to consider whether this is really the right time. Make sure there are no major events coming up in the near future that might distract you from devoting time to your new pal. Are you planning travel in the next month or two? If so, best to wait until your return. Are there any big family dates coming up, such as a wedding or a planned hospitalization? Wait until those things have happened, so you can focus on your new furry friend. If a new baby is about to arrive, give the infant your full attention—and wait until you feel you have the bandwidth for two newcomers before bringing home a "fur baby," too.

005 PREPARE FOR CUDDLES!

Some people think cats are haughty, because when they call a cat to come play (as they would a dog), some cats won't respond. The truth is that cats are just a bit more subtle than dogs, but they are generally very affectionate once they get to know you. Don't charge at a cat to say hello; instead be patient and let the cat come to you. In fact, when a cat comes close and then turns his back on you, this is often a request for a pat on the behind! Once you understand cats, they will seem much less aloof.

Most cats are very social, affectionate pets. In fact, they want to help us with a variety of our daily activities: Any cat parent who sits at a computer for any length of time knows that kitties are always willing to lend a paw or two on the keyboard, offering the ultimate in tech support! Cats love to keep you company around the home. They'll soon find your favorite room and join you there, napping while you read a book or watch TV. If you go to the bathroom, don't be surprised to find kitty is right behind you. He may even like to perch on the side of the bathtub while you wash, so take care you don't leave him unattended when the tub is full.

The point is, cats love being around us, and they love finding ways to be a part of our lives. Show a cat love and your life will always be filled with warmth, snuggles, humor, and friendship.

006 REMEMBER: FOREVER MEANS FOREVER!

When you adopt a cat, you are making a commitment to your feline friend for her entire life, just as you would a child. Get everyone together to discuss the lifestyle changes having a cat will bring about. Make sure it's understood that getting a cat is a commitment for the life of the cat, and that this can an impact on everyone's social life, travel plans, and, of course, daily routines.

NEVER GIVE A PET AS A GIFT You can't decide for someone else that they are making a commitment to care for a cat for the life of the animal. Only they can take that responsibility! A cat is not an object to be given as a gift, but a new, loving family member that needs a family who is prepared to care for her for life.

NEVER ADOPT A PET ON A WHIM We know, sometimes it really is love at first sight. But it's vital to do your research and carefully consider all the aspects and implications of adopting before you make a decision to do so. You don't want to build a bond with a cat, only to have that bond broken because you didn't think things through. You would then need to find a new home for your friend—bad news for you and for your cat.

CONSIDER WHO WILL PROVIDE CARE If you are adopting a cat for your kids, understand that the responsibility for the pet's care defaults to you. Kids, by their nature, often tire of things that were exciting when they were new, and sadly, this sometimes includes pets. Be sure you accept the possibility that you may be the one who provides most of kitty's care throughout her life.

KEEP KITTY THROUGH THICK AND THIN As awful as it sounds, animal shelters often receive cats being relinquished by people who want to "trade up" for a younger model. Remember: every adorable kitten will one day be an elderly cat who needs special attention. Be prepared to care for your pet through all of life's stages, and know that veterinarians are available to help with any bumps in the road!

007 HAVE THE TALK WITH HUMANS

Before you adopt, have a talk as a family. Make sure everyone understands the commitment you're making. A cat has needs similar to those of a child. No matter how you feel when you tumble out of bed each morning, your kitty will need fresh food and water, and a clean litter box. Unlike human children, of course, your cat will never outgrow these needs, but she will also never ask to borrow the car, nor require college funds!

THINK AHEAD Remember, a cat is not a toy that can be outgrown by children. Your cat needs a home for her entire life. If a new love interest or roommate is unwilling to accept your animals as the family members they truly are, this can create a real problem for you. Before you adopt a new cat, give serious thought to the well-being of any pets you already have, all of whom have every right to expect to live with you for their whole lives. If you have pets and you're single and you meet a new guy or girl who doesn't like cats, consider if that's really the right person for you.

ADDRESS ANY FEAR OF ANIMALS Don't assume that a child or a spouse who is terrified of cats will get over it once you adopt your new feline family member. Deal with fears before you adopt. Allow the fearful person to spend time with a friendly cat, and be patient. For help, find a psychological counselor with experience treating phobias, or read about exposure therapy online.

008 EXPLORE FAMILY HEALTH ISSUES

Does anyone in your household have a physical condition that could make it difficult to live with or care for a cat? For instance, is anyone in the family frail, blind, or in some other way unlikely to notice if a kitty happens to cross their path? Is anyone allergic to cats? An easy way to check for allergies is to spend some time in the cat section of your local shelter or visit the home of a friend who has a cat. (*See* items 009 and 010 for suggestions about how to deal with allergies.)

Some physical limitations can be easily accommodated. For example, if someone is unable to bend down to feed your cat, consider placing cat food bowls or the litter box on a table. Remember, cats are usually excellent jumpers, although older ones may need a ramp or other route up.

009 MAKE IT WORK WITH ALLERGIES!

If you know you suffer from allergies and/or asthma, make sure you check with your doctor before you adopt a cat. If you're not sure, there are some quick tests that can reveal allergies to the most common allergens, including cats.

If you are allergic to cats but still want to bring home a kitty or two, there are many things you can do to make living with a cat easier for you (*see* item 010 for some ideas). It is important that you always have preventive medications, such as fast-acting antihistamines and/or inhalers, on-hand. Keep in mind, though, that your medical condition may worsen so much that you become unable to live with a cat. For that reason, you should designate a backup pet parent who can give your kitty a forever home if necessary.

Here are a few suggestions for how you can still pursue your dream of adopting a cat while taking your allergies into consideration:

START WITH PARTIAL EXPOSURE One low-risk way to determine the severity of your allergy is to rub a paper towel on a friend's cat. Keep the paper towel around you for a few days at home and see how you react.

GENDER MAY MATTER Consider a female kitty or a male who is neutered (and has been so for several months). Skin glands that create allergens in cats are more prevalent in unaltered males. (*See* item 055.)

CONSIDER FOSTERING Many people find that over time, exposure to cats and other animals creates immunity to allergies, and their symptoms lessen. Check with your local shelter or rescue group to see if they offer a "foster-to-adopt" program. This will enable you to live with, and care for, a cat for a while, and you'll get a better idea whether your allergies will subside over time. (For more on fostering, *see* item 056.)

010 REDUCE YOUR REACTIONS

Rather than going without the joy of a cat in your life, you can take steps to reduce the allergens floating around your home and lower your reactions to them. Here are a few things to consider for starters.

Get a vacuum cleaner with a Hepa filter and vacuum frequently.

Use allergy-proof mattress covers and pillowcases.

Treat your furniture with products that neutralize the protein to which people are allergic.

Think about removing carpeting. If you have carpets, have them regularly shampooed or steamed.

Try nasal allergy-relief sprays for yourself or anti-allergy sprays for carpeting and other textiles in your home that may attract allergens.

Look at your diet—many people notice that gluten-free, dairy-free diets greatly reduce their symptoms.

Buy dust-reduced kitty litter, and maintain a clean litter box.

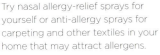

Consider investing in an air purifier machine that will remove pet dander, dust mites, mold spores, and pollen from your environment.

011

KNOW THE PET RULES WHERE YOU LIVE

While cats themselves may think rules are made to be broken, their humans are expected to pay attention to them, especially when it comes to laws governing cat ownership! Some cities have limits on the number of pets a household may contain. Generally, this is to ensure the health and safety of both humans and animals. While it's rare for local governments to intervene in cat ownership matters, they may conduct investigations if a neighbor makes complaints. Reduce the likelikhood by keeping your home clean and fresh-smelling, and you'll bring joy to both kitty and city.

IF YOU RENT Carefully read your lease to learn whether pets are allowed, and if so, how many, what type, and any size limitations. Speak to your landlord before you bring home a new cat. Sweeten the deal if needed by offering to pay a pet deposit—maybe even a bit higher than what the landlord asks for. What a show of good faith that would be! It's a good idea to get your landlord's approval, in writing, to have a cat, or at least have any language forbidding pet ownership removed from your lease.

IF YOU ARE BUYING A NEW HOME
If there is a homeowner's association, read the HOA agreement to learn about any regulations regarding pets. HOAs often place restrictions on the size or number of pets in each home. There is nothing more heartbreaking than having to decide between keeping your home or your cat. Do your due diligence before adopting a cat, as well as before choosing a new home, and everyone will be happy!

012 PREPARE FOR YOUR NEW ARRIVAL

Starting your new kitty out in his own bedroom, away from other pets (with a door you can close), will help him get used to your home gradually. While some cats may immediately strut confidently about the place like the lord of the mansion, others may feel overwhelmed at first and need a safe, quiet spot to get their bearings. Here are a few things you can do to get kitty used to the kingdom.

PROVIDE SUPPLIES Set up a filled litter box in the room and check to make sure windows and any other possible escape routes (like loose vent grills) are securely closed. Unplug or securely tape down any electrical cords, and remove any small ingestible items or anything breakable.

STOW POISONS Get rid of any dangerous items, such as coolant or antifreeze (cats love it, and it's deadly), toxic plants, human medications, and cleaning products.

Hide any toxic fluids in a garage or storage area far away from anywhere your cat may go! Remember that human medications, such as aspirin, may seem harmless, but even one pill can be fatal to your cat. Other things to keep out of your kitty's reach include batteries, seeds, and foods including grapes, raisins, and garlic (*see* item 016 for more examples). Remember: cats are very agile and can open closet doors and jump into cupboards many feet off the ground, so don't let your pet outsmart you!

"CHILDPROOF" A great way of preparing your home for your new cat is to pretend you're getting ready for a visiting (or newly arrived) baby—though one who will remain pretty much the same size throughout life. Baby-supply stores carry items to lock cupboards, cover electrical cords, and safely anchor the cords to window blinds and draperies—all good ideas to keep kitty safe.

013
CREATE KITTY'S SPACE

So, your cat's bedding, litter, food, and water are in place. Great! Now consider a few more items that she might enjoy—and add them throughout all the areas of the house where you will spend time together, such as your living room and bedroom. A cat tree is a wonderful investment. This is a piece of furniture specifically designed as a funhouse for your cat. Stabilized with a sturdy base and extending upward with a trunk that supports one or more platforms, these dandy contraptions will provide hours of exercise, snoozing opportunities, and perching zones: a playground, exercise room, napping spot, and vantage point all in one. Not to mention, as they're typically covered in carpet, they're a wonderful scratching alternative to your chic sofa!

014
SET UP A SAFE ZONE

Make sure—especially during the first week your kitty is in your home—that he has an available refuge away from everyone, including other pets (however friendly), and family members (however loving). It's all right if he hides out under a bed for a few days, as long as he is able to venture out to get to his food, water, and litter. Remember that your home offers myriad new sights, smells, and sounds and, given your kitty's incredible senses, it can be an awful lot to take in. Give him the time he needs (days or even weeks) to feel comfortable, and never scold or show disappointment towards him if he needs just a little longer to feel safe. This is a new world for him, and some cats may need more time to settle in. He may prefer his own litter box to a shared one, for example, and, during this introduction period, he is much better off being able to eat and drink from his own bowls in an area away from other pets. Generally speaking, kitties will begin to feel confident in their surroundings within a week—but if it's longer, don't panic. Sooner or later, you'll be able to cuddle up happily at home together.

015 REMOVE CHOKING HAZARDS

Even after you've done a once-over for items that pose a threat to your cat's well-being, it's worth refining your search for potential dangers in your home. As you focus, you'll see more things you'll want to keep away from kitty. Among the small objects to store safely are rubber bands, safety pins, needles, thread, paper clips, staples, small erasers and those on the end of pencils, coins, and bottle caps. Even earplugs may be ingested and cause intestinal blockage. Remember, cats are excellent jumpers and very curious so placing these items on high shelves is not enough! Shut them away in closed drawers and cupboards, safely out of your kitty's reach.

016 STOW AWAY TOXINS

Among the poisonous items that you need to keep away from kitty are human medications, including vitamins and supplements. Although acetaminophen, adult aspirin, or ibuprofen may seem harmless, even one pill can be fatal for your cat.

Small batteries, seeds of all kinds and fruit pits, paint, and paint thinners, pesticides, glue, tinsel, and tobacco are all harmful to cats. Also, foods such as grapes, raisins, garlic, onion, coffee, tea and other caffeinated foods, chocolate, mushrooms, walnuts, yeast, and hops can be toxic to all pets, so keep these items in sealed containers behind securely closed doors!

017 STOCK SAFE SNACKS

Ever encounter a kitty munching on grass, and thought it was silly? The truth is that some grasses are very good for cats. The most common kitty grasses are *Avena sativa* and *Dactylis glomerata*. Although they sound somewhat like fanciful Harry Potter characters, the first is an oat and the second is more commonly known as orchard grass or cocksfoot. Other beneficial kitty grasses include barley, flax, and wheatgrass.

GROW YOUR OWN Cat grass seeds can be found in pet and gardening supply stores, as well as in the pet food sections of some grocery stores. Cat grass is easily grown inside on a sunny window (and also outside, weather permitting). Keep in mind that cats can overindulge in cat grass, so you may not want to make it available to kitty 24/7. Bring it out as a treat for a few minutes a day.

PROVIDE THE NUTRIENTS Cat grass aids your kitty's digestion, and it can help move hairballs through her digestive tract. It may lead to vomiting, which is not a bad thing in this case, as that can also help eliminate hairballs. Certain nutrients in cat grass are very good for your cat and aren't necessarily found in her other food. For dentally challenged kitties or those who don't seem interested in chomping on a cat plant, try snipping blades into half-inch (1-cm) pieces and mix a teaspoon or so into wet food.

018 AVOID THE DANGERS

The cat's instinct to chew plants can cause problems since a number of common garden and house plants are potentially dangerous to cats.

Listed below are some plants to keep out of kitty's way. If he ingests a bite of an off-limits plant, look for one of these symptoms of toxicity: vomiting, diarrhea, increased heart rate, drooling, a lack of coordination,

or even just a hint of a seizure or actually falling unconscious. If you see any of these things or you are at all concerned, take him to a vet immediately!

Believe it or not, even realistic-looking plastic plants may attract your kitty enough that he takes a bite. If he's at all interested in an artificial plant, move it to a place where he can't snack on it!

BAD FOR CATS

• Aloe vera	• Daffodil	• Kalanchoe	• Oleander	• Sweet pea
• Azalea	• Fern	• Leek	• Passionflower	• Tulip
• Castor bean	• Geranium	• Lily	• Peony	• Virginia creeper
• Chrysanthemum	• Holly	• Marijuana	• Poinsettia	• Golden trumpet
• Crocus	• Ivy (many)	• Morning glory	• Primrose	• Wisteria
• Cyclamen	• Jasmine	• Narcissus	• Sago palm	• Yew

019 STOCK UP ON SUPPLIES

A new addition to the family will require certain key items for her health, happiness, and well-being. Here are a few things to stock up on before you bring kitty home for the first time—or a few things to grab once you've gotten her settled in.

COLLAR & TAG Get a tag (online or in a pet store) with your cell number engraved as large as possible. If your's is an indoors-only cat have a second tag that says "I'm lost" incase he gets out (*see* items 068–069). Get your cat microchipped (*see* item 067) and you'll have another tag with the cat's microchip ID number for tracking purposes.if needed.

BOWLS If you have more than one cat, it's generally a good idea to offer each cat their food in a separate bowl. However, most cats don't mind sharing a single water bowl.

DRY & WET FOOD Dry food is more convenient than wet food because it takes less space to store, it is less odorous, and you don't have to worry about recycling cans. But wet food contains more moisture, which your cat needs. Dry food also contains more carbohydrates, and these can contribute to your cat becoming overweight if you overfeed him. Most vets recommend a balance of both wet and dry food.

TOYS Cats can enjoy stuffed mice covered with faux fur, springs with balls attached, wires with teaser toys at the end, chase track toys (a ball in an open tunnel that cats can try to catch), kitty crawl tunnels, cat trees, homemade toys, and many more.

BRUSH & FLEA COMB Cats like to groom themselves, but they can also like having a gentle stroke with a brush. A flea comb is a must-have tool that you can use occasionally to determine if your cats are carrying fleas. Dark specks on the comb are flea droppings.

FLEA CONTROL PRODUCT Topical or not, defend against pests.

BEDDING While cats can create their own lounging area, sometimes in the strangest places, if you want to keep cat hair off furniture, a dedicated cat bed is a fine thing.

LITTER BOXES One litter box per cat is recommended. Many people (and cats) prefer hooded boxes, which offer privacy and help contain odors.

020 PROVIDE ENTERTAINMENT

Enriching your cat's environment with things to stimulate and entertain her will keep her active and content. When cats are bored, they may turn to chewing on household items, knocking small objects off mantles to create something interesting to watch, or other destructive behaviors, or they may just become sedentary, gain weight, and be generally unhappy.

You can keep your cat happy and stimulated with a few simple home hacks. Even something as simple as providing a cat with a comfortable resting spot near an open, screened-in window with a view can add excitement to her day. Add a bird feeder outside that window and she will really perk up and have something interesting to watch! Some cats enjoy TV, and there are even DVDs specifically designed for cats.

Cats are natural jumpers and climbers. They will jump onto shelves, counter tops, windowsills, or any furniture. Many cats enjoy cat trees they can climb. Placing two cat trees a few feet away from each other provides a good jumping challenge. Catwalks (high shelves that run the length of your walls) are an great way to give your cat a place to jump to. Many cats also enjoy quiet cubbyholes to hide and snooze in. You might consider dedicating one shelf in a linen closet for your cat to snuggle on. Just make sure the closet door is always open so your cat can't get trapped inside.

021 GET THE TOYS!

There's no doubt about it: Active cats are healthier, both mentally and physically. Indoor cats especially need the stimulation of interactive toys and it's a great idea to play along. Playing with your cat will help you to bond quickly, and there are plenty of toys that will provide hours of fun when you're not available.

Kitty-approved favorites include all types of toys that suspend on a doorknob or are mounted in a floor stand, such as springs with balls on the end, safely wound wire with cardboard "chews" attached, mini lasers (do not point at anyone's eyes), stuffed plush toys, and any balls that roll, bounce, jingle, squeak, and squish.

But keep in mind that you might splash out on some pricey toy mice, an elegant bed, and an expensive cat tree for Scooter McFluff, only to find out that Scooter prefers balled-up pieces of paper, the laundry basket,

and some old shoes you keep meaning to get rid of. Cats can be very inexpensive to entertain, as these DIY toys prove (*see* also items 169–171).

PING-PONG BALLS Ping-pong balls have just the right amount of bounce to be loads of fun. Be sure to rinse off any factory residue before playtime.

PAPER TOWEL ROLLS Cardboard rolls from paper towels and bathroom tissue offer free, recycled fun.

CARDBOARD BOXES Plain cardboard boxes or paper grocery bags are an old standby. (Remove bag handles as paws could get caught in them.) You can even tape and stack cardboard boxes together and cut passageways to create a maze for your kitty to explore!

022 USE LITTER BOX LOGIC

Besides fresh water, food, and a safe home, the most basic thing you need to provide your cat is a clean litter box or pan. There are many options in terms of types of boxes and types of litter, but here are the basic rules:

KEEP IT CLEAN! Cats are usually happy to use a litter box, which is essentially a toilet you provide, but they need you to flush that toilet once a day. Scoop out all feces and urine clumps, and follow the disposal instructions for the type of litter you have chosen. This is usually flushing it down your toilet or wrapping it securely and placing it in your trashcan, but ensure you don't contravene local regulations. Every month empty out the old litter, sanitize the pan with soap and hot water, then fill it with new litter.

KEEP IT QUIET Make sure the litter box location is conducive for your cat's use. Try to keep it away from a high-traffic area in your home. After all, this is your feline friend's private bathroom. If you want to conceal the box for aesthetic purposes and your style of box has a top, you can cover the top with a nice cloth (leaving open the box entrance). Or you can place the box in a closet or cabinet, but make sure the door can never close, and that the spot has plenty of ventilation.

MAKE IT BIG Regardless of the number of kitties, the bigger the box, the better. You may need to have a small box due to space limitations or if you have young kittens, but from your cat's point of view, usually bigger is better.

TOP IT UP Keep the litter box topped up. Typically, litter three inches (7 cm) deep is ideal. This helps contain odors, and is more appealing to kitty, whose digging and burying instincts are better served with more material to scratch around in. Putting in too much litter can cause it to spill out as your cat tries to bury what she is leaving behind.

023 EXPLORE YOUR OPTIONS

There are many different options available to you and your kitty, from simple low pans—often a good place to start with small kittens—to high-end electronic self-cleaning boxes. Here are a few to think about:

A DESIGNER COMMODE Pet supply stores carry a vast array of colors and designs, and you can find custom-made wooden and woven litter box covers on the internet that can turn a litter box into a beautiful piece of furniture.

SELF-CLEANING BOX "Scoop-free" litter boxes reduce your daily work. The non-electronic variety involves rolling the box so that waste falls through a grill into a separate compartment that you remove and empty. The electronic variety rakes or sweeps waste into the separate compartment after your cat leaves the box. Sensors reset the rake or sweeper whenever your cat reenters the box. Of course, this is the priciest option. Some cats get scared by the automatic motion, so it is not for everyone.

A HOOD IS GOOD A litter box with a hood or lid will provide your cat with privacy, and it will hide the litter pan from human view, as well. It will also help contain odor and hold in the litter so you have less sweeping up to do if your cat tends to kick litter out of the box.

VARY THE OPTIONS Households with numerous cats may find that variety is helpful for kitties—having several litter boxes in the home, and even offering hooded or electronic vs. open pan varieties may be a good way to go.

USE A MAT Whatever litter box option you use, consider having a mat in the spot where your cat enters and exits. Special litter box mats encourage any litter trapped between your cat's toes to fall off, decreasing the amount of litter your cat may track out of the box and around your house.

AN OPEN PAN Some kitties may have trouble stepping up into a high box. If this is the case, or if you have limited room (or a pint-sized kitten), you can opt for a simple, uncovered pan. It won't provide privacy, of course, and it will lack the partial odor-cloaking properties of a hooded box. But it may reduce stress for a kitty that is prone to urgent rushes to eliminate, and for elderly or frail cats.

024 CATPROOF YOUR FURNITURE

Because of your cat's heightened senses, she can discern your personal scent on everything you touch, including your furniture. If you like your sofa, so will she, even when you're not on it. As far as kitty is concerned, it's her furniture, too—so here's how to do a little cat-proofing and keep it looking nice.

TOSS A THROW
Draping an inexpensive throw blanket across furniture is a simple way to keep cat hair in one, easily-removable place.

TRY BUMPY MATS
Plastic mats with raised bumps (sold in pet stores) can deter your cat from leaping onto the furniture. She may also stay off it even after you've removed the mats.

ADD SOME CITRUS
Spraying citrusy smells on your cat's favorite parts of your furniture may deter her from lounging there. Just be sure whatever you spray is safe for your cat and your furniture alike.

OFFER CHOICES
Give your cat plenty of nice, cushiony spots to sit, ideally elevated and close to windows for his viewing pleasure. The goal is to make better spots available—so he'll want to spend less time on that boring old sofa. As with any training, reward your cat with verbal accolades, treats, snuggles, and brushing when he's learned what you expect of him regarding the furniture. This will reinforce his behavior—and keep you happy.

025 KEEP SCRATCHING AT BAY

If your cat is tempted to scratch your furniture (as most are), try these tips:

- Keep your cat's nails trimmed (*see* item 202 for details on how to handle this task safely). This is the foolproof way to keep your furniture (and you and other pets) safe from scratches.

- Affix clear, double-sided tape strips to the sides of any chair or sofa your cat is tempted to scratch. Because she'll associate scratching here with getting her paws stuck, she may no longer consider it such a desirable spot—even after you remove the tape.

- Put a scratching post or mat in front of the favored piece of furniture. Your cat might get the message and use the designated item.

- Invest in plastic or vinyl claw caps to cover your cat's sharp claws. Cats generally don't mind them, and the caps' dull ends prevent claws from penetrating fabric and other surfaces.

026

GET ALERTED!

Cats can hear much better than humans. In fact, the slightest perception of sound can pull a cat out of a deep slumber. Your cat may know if someone is approaching your home or trying to break in before you can hear it. He may not be able to pick up the phone and call the police, but seeing your cat bolt across your path may warn you that something is not right.

027 GO TO BED

Not only will bringing home "Mr. Wiggles" change your lifestyle during the day, but your nighttime routine can be affected as well.

GET TO KNOW KITTY'S HABITS Determine whether you plan to share your bedroom with your new family member. If you do, keep in mind that he may live up to his name and wiggle, snore, claim more than his share of the bed, or even pounce on your feet. Or he could be the ideal bed buddy, snoozing peacefully all night. Many people find the few minutes they spend with a cat before sleep and after waking is ideal bonding time.

LET KITTY SLEEPWALK You probably don't sleep two-thirds of your day, but many cats do—and then become more active at night. Your cat may want to do a little exploring during some of the evening hours, when your home is still (or when other critters, such as mice and bugs, might be stirring in your walls). There might be some interesting raccoons or outdoor cats passing by outside to watch, or some fascinating headlights rushing by. So even if he snuggles up in the bedroom when you head to bed, keep your door open to allow him the chance to roam. He'll thank you for it—and hopefully you can sleep through any scampering.

028 PLAN FOR TRAVEL

We cover much more about travel in the CARE section, but as you consider getting a new cat, keep in mind that if everyone in your household plans to travel at the same time, you'll need to find a pet sitter to care for your feline family member while you are all away. Your sitter will either need to stay at your house (they can water the plants while they're at it), or visit at least once a day to feed and check on your cat. If you're only headed off for the weekend, you might not need an overnight sitter. But if you're leaving for more than two nights, it's a good idea.

LET KITTY STAY HOME Since cats prefer as little disruption in their lives as possible, it's best to let them stay at home when you're away, rather than boarding them. If your cat can stay home, he won't have to deal with the stress of travel, a new environment, and new

people catering to his needs, all of which can be very traumatic for a cat (much more so than for a dog). An ideal sitter can be a friend or family member who already knows your cat. Neighbors who can stop by each day to feed, freshen water, and check on your cat can work out well. You can also pay for a professional cat sitter, but be sure to fully research and interview them to make sure they are trustworthy.

BOARD IF YOU MUST If you really can't find someone reliable to care for your cat at your house, it is possible to find pleasant and cozy boarding facilities with loving staff. If you opt to board your kitty, research prospective facilities as much as possible, just as you would a home sitter. Visit the facility you're considering, check online reviews, and, if you can, get references from trusted friends and acquaintances.

029 FIGURE OUT BASIC COSTS

Before you adopt, take an inventory of the expenses you'll likely incur. If you buy everything brand-new, plan on spending a pretty penny for supplies, in addition to your adoption fee. You may be able to cut some of these costs by shopping frugally, borrowing some supplies, or improvising things like bedding and toys.

Depending on where you adopt, there are some costs you might have up-front or you might avoid. For example, if you adopt from a shelter or rescue group your new cat may already be spayed or neutered, which will save you this expense. If not, however, you will need to factor in spaying or neutering your cat as your vet recommends (this procedure can be done safely when a kitten is as young as eight weeks old). Also, initial vaccines may have been given to a cat you adopt from a shelter or rescue group.

Here is a quick list of the items you should expect to obtain right away and those that you'll need to budget for on a regular basis for the life of your pet:

UP-FRONT COSTS

- Food and bowls
- Litter, litter box, scooper
- Bedding
- Toys
- Collar and tag
- Microchip implant, if your cat doesn't already have one (see item 067)
- Initial vet visit, even if you've gotten your cat from a shelter
- License (rarely required, but check in your area)
- Brush
- Scratching posts or boards
- Tick and flea preventative treatment (ask your vet)

ONGOING COSTS

- Food
- Cat litter
- Regular vet visits
- Pet health insurance (see item 154)
- Pet sitting while you travel
- Tick and flea preventative treatment
- Toys

030 FACTOR IN UNEXPECTED EXPENSES

Figuring out how much you would spend on your pet in an emergency is a tough and very personal decision. These costs will vary according to your cat's medical condition, and which veterinarian you use. One important way to be sure you can provide needed medical care for your cat is to purchase pet health insurance. For a small monthly fee, you will have the peace of mind that much of your cat's medical bill will be covered if she has to undergo expensive procedures down the road.

031 PRICE PET SITTERS UP FRONT

If you are likely to need to have someone else look after your cat on a regular basis, or just for the odd vacation, be sure to check you can afford it before adopting. Depending on where you live, pet sitters charge between $15–25 USD per visit and more for in-home sitting where veterinary support, such as administering medications, is required. If medication or vet tech support is not required, pet sitters that will stay overnight may only charge $50–60 USD a day, depending on where you live. (For more on sitters, *see* items 179–185.)

If you opt to board your kitty, the cost will usually begin at around $20 USD per cat per day. This may not include food (which you would provide), medications, and any other special support your cat may require.

032
CONSIDER AN INDOOR CAT

Depending on where you live, you may see cats wandering freely outdoors. These may be feral cats who are living in alleyways surviving off food they scavenge, or they may be cats who have loving homes and who are allowed access to go both indoors and outdoors. While it can be reasonably safe to have an outdoor cat in some areas, statistics show that cats who are kept indoors live longer and healthier lives. If you decide to keep your cat indoors, however, you do need to provide all his entertainment.

FEWER DANGERS Being outdoors presents many hazards for a cat, which contributes to the statistical likelihood of a shorter lifespan. Some of the risk factors include:
• Being struck by a car
• Predators, such as coyotes, who may injure or kill domestic cats
• Poor treatment by a cruel person
• Fights and injuries from other cats, dogs, raccoons, and other wildlife or neighbor pets
• Poisons your cat can ingest
• Overeating or being fed unhealthy food by well-meaning neighbors
• Communicable diseases such as FIV

MORE FUN! Cats enjoy having things to watch and chase. For indoor cats, this is often best accomplished by having more than one cat or having a cat-friendly dog, so they can interact and play with each other. Also, setting up windowsill perches and leaving screened windows open so your cat can observe and smell the outdoors are great ideas. And of course, toys, particularly those that move unpredictably or make sounds, can be really fun for your cat.

033 PREPARE FOR THE GREAT OUTDOORS

If you are adopting a cat who has already been living outdoors, she may be perfectly happy, and even relieved, to now have a safe indoor environment. But there are cases where a cat who has lived outside is unhappy staying indoors, and demonstrates this by howling beside the door, or even spraying or urinating indoors.

If this happens, you should first do all you can to make the indoor environment as stimulating as possible. If, however, you have decided that your cat is truly unhappy and you want to give her the opportunity to go outdoors, you can create a safe outdoor enclosure (*see* item 205), and that will likely do the trick!

If you don't have the space for an enclosure and your cat is still visibly unhappy, and you're willing to accept the risks of letting her wander outside (including the chance of her being taken in by a stranger, being painfully injured or even killed, and potentially high medical bills in case of disease or injury), here is what you must do:

DOOR Install a cat door in a back door or window so your cat can come back inside as and when she pleases.

EXIT Only allow your cat out through a back door or window that leads to a yard or somewhere where there are no cars. It's crucial that you train your cat to stay away from the street, and close to your backyard.

MICROCHIP Be sure your little friend has a microchip and your information is up to date in the microchip registry. If you're not sure your cat has a microchip, ask your veterinarian to scan her and, if a chip is detected, to tell you which registry to contact with your information.

TAG Put a tag on her collar that says, "Please do NOT feed me." You can't control your cat's diet and health when other people are feeding her different types and amounts of food without your knowledge.

PLEASE DO **NOT** FEED ME

COLLAR Put a collar with identification, including your cell number, on your cat. Make it a stretchy one so he has wiggle out room if the collar gets snagged on something. In fact, buy several collars and tags in advance, so if the collar gets lost, you can replace it! Never allow your pet outdoors without identification. If something happens to him, someone will need his ID to be able contact you.

MEALS Only feed your cat inside. This will help train him to come home for meals, assuming neighbors don't feed your cat when he's out and about.

034 KEEP COWS IN BARNS AND CATS ON COUCHES

Some people have cats simply for rodent control in barns or outside areas. While some animal shelters have barnyard cat programs as a last resort for sterilized feral cats who cannot be domesticated, this is not the ideal life for a domesticated companion animal unless you have the guidance of counselors at an animal shelter

There are many ways cats can come to harm on farms. They may drink toxic fluid from leaky vehicle radiators or eat old rat poison or other fatal substances. If a cat catches a rat, the rat might be carrying disease or may have recently ingested a poison that will be

transferred to the cat. Mousetraps, raccoons, predators, and many other factors can spell disaster for your kitty around a barnyard. If you want to keep rodents out of your buildings, your best resort is to seal all holes in doors and walls, remove, tightly seal, or otherwise safely store all potential foods, and then use humane traps to capture and relocate rodents outside. To prevent reinfestation, use non-toxic rodent repellents such as peppermint oil, or plug in high-frequency sound devices that are not audible to human ears (but make sure your dog is never in close proximity to such a device).

035 DON'T SHOP— ADOPT!

So you're ready to add some fluff and fun in your life, and you have a little free time in the coming weeks? No pressing engagements or major upcoming life events? Fantastic! The time is right!

ENRICH A LIFE When you adopt a cat from an animal shelter or rescue organization, you save a life while enriching your own. Thank you in advance for doing this wonderful thing! In most cases, you also get the benefit of adopting a kitten or cat who has been spayed or neutered, vaccinated, microchipped, dewormed, rid of fleas, given a medical exam, and even tested for diseases such as FIV and FeLV (see more in the HEALTH section).

ADOPT ONE AND SAVE ANOTHER The story of pet overpopulation in animal shelters is a very sad one: millions of animals that do not have homes are killed each year in the United States alone. When you adopt a cat or kitten, you are freeing up space in the shelter or rescue organization for more cats to have a chance at life as well. And, because your cat will be spayed or neutered, you will help prevent the suffering of future generations of unwanted kittens.

036 CHECK YOUR LOCAL SHELTER

Your local animal shelter is likely to have a variety of adoptable kitties available. Although it's good to bring the whole family to the shelter to meet your prospective new family member, it can be hard, especially on young children, to leave so many pets behind after the visit, knowing that the family can't adopt them all. Consider visiting the shelter by yourself first. When you return with children, introduce them to the one or two lucky kitties you feel may be the best fit for your family.

ASK FOR PLAY TIME Animal shelters want to find permanent, loving homes for their animals, so feel free to ask for ample time to explore, look at, and talk to the kitties. You may even be able to pet or hold them. Again, remember not to overwhelm a child with choices, and not to overwhelm a cat with too much petting when she is stressed and doesn't yet know or trust you.

PAY THE ADOPTION FEE WITH GLEE! Once you've selected your cat or kitten at a shelter, you'll need to complete some paperwork. This is an important step in ensuring that you (and the shelter) are comfortable with the adoption. You'll most likely be asked to pay an adoption fee. Adoption fees vary greatly, and may range from $20–200 USD or more. The fee provides much-needed support for the shelter and the pets it cares for, and it's likely a bargain, since the shelter may have already spayed or neutered your cat and provided her with numerous medical services. You may even receive free samples of food and coupons for pet supplies as well.

CONSIDER A PRIVATE RESCUE Another way to adopt is through a private non-profit group such as a humane society that has a shelter facility, or a rescue group that houses its pets in foster homes and displays them at weekend adoption events, often at pet supply stores. The process of adopting your kitty will be similar to that of a shelter, but a rescuer may also wish to visit your home before you adopt, in order to evaluate it for safety and suitability. This can be good for you, as the rescuer may have helpful suggestions. While adopting from a rescue group may be a more complex process than adoption from a public shelter, and often more expensive, one advantage is that the rescue group will likely have more hands-on information on the background and behavior of the cats in its care, and know something of each one's character, too.

037 START ONLINE

Did you know that you can use Adopt-a-Pet.com or Petfinder.com to start your search for your new best friend? Local rescue groups, humane societies, and animal shelters post their pets for adoption on these sites, which allow you to search for a pet by using criteria such as breed, gender, color, and other options. You can even sign up to be alerted when the type of cat you are seeking gets posted. It's fun and free, and there's also plenty of helpful advice to help you prepare for adoption and acclimate your new pet into your life.

038 ADOPT FROM FRIENDS OR FAMILY

If someone you know has found a homeless cat or perhaps needs to find a new home for their own cat due to unfortunate circumstances in their life, this may be that rare situation where you can get to know a cat before you adopt. You can spend time getting comfortable with your prospective adoptee before you bring him home. In the case of a person who can no longer keep their cat, you can also get lots of information about the cat's behaviors and medical history, all of which can help make the adoption a success.

039 IF SO SMITTEN, CHOOSE A KITTEN

What's the one thing that doesn't exist anywhere in the universe? An uncute kitten! Those giant eyes, itty-bitty noses, fat bellies, wild leaps, and sideways pounces—kittens are adorable! But it's important to remember that they're a good deal of work, too.

Like all babies, kittens are still learning about life and their environment. They're also refining their motor skills: That's a fancy way of saying they're enthusiastic slobs. This means your kitten may knock over or decimate houseplants, turn his food and water bowls into disaster areas, and get soggy cat litter everywhere. Understand that this will happen, and ask yourself if you can handle it without becoming stressed. Cats are quick learners. But they're also sensitive to stress, so if you can manage cleanup with joy, you'll have a joyful cat! If, on the other hand, the whole process makes you tense, your kitten will also feel uptight, and this can affect his health and your future relationship with him.

040 CATER TO A KITTEN

There are a few kitten behaviors that require ironing out and some special approaches that cats need when they're young. Here are a few things you can do to ensure smooth sailing in the early days of adoption.

RESOLVE SCRATCHING ISSUES Learning to safely trim your kitten's claws (*see* item 202) is a great way to begin protecting things in your home from being scratched. It's also OK to put vinyl nail caps on your kitten's claws. Follow the instructions carefully, or get help from your vet or groomer, and make sure your kitten doesn't try to eat them. If that happens, no more nail caps! Whatever you do, do not declaw your cat. This is a painful and unnecessary amputation of the ends of her toes.

MANAGE MIDNIGHT MADNESS Even though cats sleep up to 18 hours a day, they may want to blast around in the middle of the night, especially if they aren't stimulated enough during the day. Adopting a pair of kittens is a good way to reduce wild nighttime behavior, as they'll often play each other to sleep. While adult cats may already have developed the habit of sleeping

through the night, kittens and cats who are new to your home may need time to learn or relearn this.

TRAIN. SOCIALIZE. REPEAT. Kittens need a lot of socializing to grow into well-adjusted, friendly adults. A kitten that is left alone while you work long hours may become withdrawn or overly needy. The simplest solution is to adopt two kittens, or make sure your kitten has an adult feline pal. If that isn't possible, be sure to shower a lot of attention on your kitten when you're home, and avoid taking overnight trips while she is under a year old, or arrange for a cat sitter to keep her company if you do. A general rule of thumb is that you can leave a four-week-old kitten alone for two hours at a time, and a little longer when you have two kittens. Arranging for a loving person to visit your kitten while you're at work can also reassure them.

FOSTER FIRST If you're not sure whether you can devote the time to raise a kitten, consider fostering. If your local shelter has kittens too young to be adopted, staff will welcome a volunteer to care for them until they can be spayed or neutered and adopted out to a new home. This will help the shelter and give you a kitten test run (*see* also item 056).

041 UNDERSTAND TRAP-NEUTER-RETURN

If you find cats living in a relatively safe area (such as a field or small alley), it is tempting, as a cat lover, to start bringing them food or water. SImply doing that can cause them to become healthier (which is good) but then produce more kittens (which is bad).

The ideal way to help these cats is manage them using a system called trap-neuter-return (TNR). This means setting out humane traps then bringing the trapped cat to a veterinarian to be spayed or neutered and receive vaccinations. The cat will then be marked with a small notch at the edge of the cat's ear to indicate she has been sterilized, and when she has fully recovered she can be released where she was found.

If you find kittens, it may make better sense not to return the kittens where you found them, but instead socialize them and find them good homes.

042   SALVE A LOST KITTEN

SAVE A LOST KITTEN

If you come across a kitten that looks like he is still young enough to be nursing (under four or five weeks old), don't just assume the kitten is abandoned. Look around for the kitten's mom. She may be off getting food or water and will return shortly. If you see her, let the kitten stay with mom. This is a great time, though, to contact your local humane society organization or a rescue group and see if they do feral colony maintenance. This means someone might come and trap the cats in the area, get them spayed or neutered and up-to-date on shots, and then released back into the environment where they can live, but not reproduce.

If the mother cat doesn't appear, come back in a couple of hours to see if the kitten is still there. If there is still no sign of mom, it may be that she has been injured or even killed. Call your local cat rescue organization to get their advice. They may say it is best for you to care for the kitten yourself, if you can, by providing food and medical attention and eventually finding her a permanent loving home.

If you have taken in a kitten from off the street, immediately isolate your new friend safely indoors, away from children and other pets, preferably in a bathroom. Put tape over any nearby exposed wall outlets in case kittens are tempted to insert curious tiny paws. Don't leave kittens outdoors, and if you must use a garage (which should only be a last resort), be sure there are no harmful insects or spiders living in it, and pack away all hazardous chemicals, such as antifreeze (*see* item 016).

043 CARE FOR THE BABY

Kittens need to be bottle fed until they are about five to eight weeks old. Cow's milk may soothe their hunger, but it lacks the nutrition they need, and may cause diarrhea. Goat's milk is better. Feed the milk with a plastic syringe or eyedropper. An emergency litter box can be made from a cardboard box and some shredded newspaper.

As soon as possible, get to a pet supply store and buy some kitten milk replacement (find the right formula for the kitten's age). You will also need a small plastic baby bottle for each kitten. While there look for a plastic litter pan about three inches (7 cm) high and some non-clumping kitty litter (kittens may eat clumping litter, which can be life-threatening).

044 COOK UP A SUBSTITUTE

If you can't immediately get to a pet supply store, you can put together a DIY formula substitute to tide kitty over. You will need: a package of unflavored gelatin, one egg yolk, a tablespoon of light, non-GMO corn syrup, two tablespoons of plain yogurt, two tablespoons of mayonnaise, and one twelve-ounce (354-ml) can of evaporated milk. Follow the instructions below. Cool the formula to a comfortable temperature before feeding using a plastic baby bottle, eyedropper, or syringe. The formula will last for several days if refrigerated.

STEP ONE
Gather together the ingredients, a large bowl, and a clean spoon. Boil a kettleful of water.

STEP TWO
Use some of the boiling water to dissolve the gelatin as directed on the package.

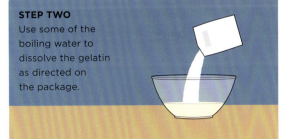

STEP THREE
Use more boiling water to sterilize the spoon and the bottles, eyedroppers, or syringes.

STEP FOUR
Add all the other ingredients to the gelatine and blend well.

045 BE A BOTTLE BABY EXPERT

Feeding a young kitten takes a while to master. There are a few techniques that will help you ensure your bottle baby gets all the food she needs to grow and be healthy.

PERFECT YOUR METHOD Using sterilized scissors, make a small X on the baby bottle nipple to allow for easy, even flow. Follow the formula directions for mixing a feed (or make your own, *see* item 044), and fill the bottle. Before you feed, gently hug your kitten in a towel until any shivering stops. The best feeding position for a kitten is on all fours with her head slightly raised. Gently squeeze the bottle (syringe or dripper) as the kitten

drinks. The amount of formula a kitten needs depends on her weight. (She should be gaining weight daily, so the quantity should increase daily.) A kitten should eat about eight milliliters per ounce (28 gm) of bodyweight per day, over several feeds. So, a kitten who weighs five ounces (125 gm) should eat around 40 milliliters of formula each day. Depending upon the kitten, you may be giving as many as eight feeds a day. Divide the total food per day by eight to determine how much to give each time.

GET A CHECK UP If your kitten always seems hungry, even after feeding, see your vet to make sure she is healthy. In fact, it's best to regularly consult your vet about feeding schedules before your kitten is old enough for solid wet food (generally at four to five weeks of age). You want to be sure she is getting enough nutrition, but overfeeding can be dangerous, especially if a kitten has elimination problems. It's a delicate balance. Ask your vet a lot of questions and ask for help if you need it.

046
TAKE TINKLE TIME

With a very young kitten, you need to imitate what his mother would do and encourage him to eliminate. Each day, after one of his feedings, dip a soft, clean cloth in warm water and gently rub your kitten's private parts from front to back to stimulate going to the bathroom. When the kitten begins to eliminate, place him in the litter to get him used to using the litter box. If twenty-four hours pass without any pee or poop, take him to the vet to rule out a medical issue. Once you begin to see your kitten use the litter box on his own, you can stop the stimulation. Just be sure he is tinkling at least once a day!

047 SLEEP SOUNDLY

While a kitten is nursing, you may want to bury a ticking wind-up clock (make sure the alarm is off) in her bedding to simulate the beating of her mother's heart. A hot water bottle nestled in the bedding is also much appreciated. The coziest spot for kitten is on your lap, but if you want to snuggle, sit on a low bed or cushion, so there's no risk of falling! And remember not to lie next to a sleeping kitten if there is a risk you might doze off and roll onto her.

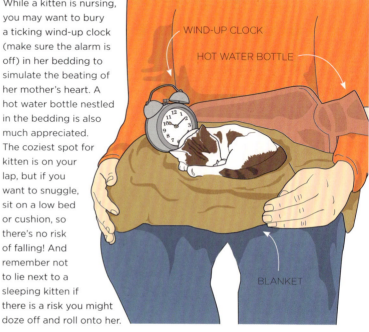

WIND-UP CLOCK

HOT WATER BOTTLE

BLANKET

048 BRING HOME AN ADULT (OR TWO!)

If you want a cat in your life but don't have the time, energy, or patience to teach a kitten how to use the litter box or stop ravaging shoes and plants, an adult cat is a great way to go, and shelters are filled with them! Adult cats tend to settle into routines quickly, making them great housemates.

One thing to consider is that sometimes, due to changes in a pet parent's life, two adult cats who are used to living together are surrendered to a shelter at the same time. Shelters and rescuers sometimes call these bonded pairs, since they're already comfortable with each other. Imagine their joy at being adopted and staying together. Having each other as company will make their adjustment into a new home easier, and you'll soon enjoy two relaxed, happy cats who seem like they've lived with you all along!

049 ADOPT A SENIOR IN NEED

Adopting a senior kitty is a wonderful thing. As with any pet in a shelter, the senior is there through no fault of his own. Perhaps the cat's previous human was also elderly, and had to move to a care facility that didn't accept pets. Or maybe this senior cat needed age-related medical procedures or medication that their first parent just couldn't afford. Or, in some very sad cases, an owner may may have discarded an older cat at a shelter to be replaced by a younger pet.

While that's awful news, here's the flip side! A senior kitty in a shelter or with a rescue organization is far more likely to already be trained and housebroken, and should be calmer, than a younger cat. And he'll be more than thrilled to once again have a home of his own, so he may adapt more quickly.

There are advantages to adopting mature animals. You already know what their personality will be for the rest of their lives, and senior pets are much less likely to chew your favorite pair of shoes or shred your couch or curtains than a wild young kitten.

050 MAKE A STRAY'S DAY!

If you spot a cat outside who seems content and unafraid of people, this is likely an indoor-outdoor cat from a nearby home in the neighborhood, and all may be well. If your instincts tell you that the cat shouldn't be there, particularly if she seems distressed or disorientated, patiently call her to you (using food if you have it to lure her close) and see if she has a collar and tag with a phone number to call. The poor kitty may be lost.

If there's no tag with contact info, and you suspect that the cat is lost or abandoned, take her to a veterinarian to have her scanned for a microchip. Also, look around the area for posted signs about a missing cat, and check online lost-pet registries to see if this cat's description matches any reported cases. If your local laws do not require this, it may be best to avoid taking the cat to a shelter. Many shelters are overcrowded and if she isn't claimed within a few days, she may be euthanized or relocated. But do ask shelters if you can put up "found cat" posters to make it easy for an owner to contact you, since someone who has lost a cat may go to the shelter as part of their search.

051 UNDERSTAND FERAL CATS

If you see a kitty who seems afraid of people it may be a feral cat. Feral is the description given to a cat who was born on the street and has never lived with or been socialized by humans. Feral cats typically remain fearful of humans for their whole lives and will most likely run away if approached.

Hopefully, the cat is in good health, and is part of a managed feral colony, where he is given food, water, and even shelter by a kindhearted citizen. If the cat's ear is tipped (the top of one ear has been notched), this cat is probably a spayed or neutered feral. The ear tip lets other feral caretakers know that there is no need to trap the cat for sterilization. These cats have also likely been vaccinated and tested for communicable diseases. If you're concerned that

the cat may not be well, report to your local humane society or rescue organization right away.

Even if you mean well, the worst thing you can do is capture a feral cat in hopes of taming him, only to have him run away, scared, into a strange environment. Unable to again find the colony where he lived, he will be left to roam, frightened and alone, with no access to food and water.

Taming a feral cat, even a kitten, is not something to attempt without seeking advice from someone who has successfully accomplished this in the past. Feral cats brought to public shelters are often euthanized right away because they are not considered adoptable. So, if you want to try to tame and adopt a feral cat, seek the advice of a cat rescue organization!

052 KNOW YOUR BASIC BREEDS

While particular dog breeds often share some general character traits, this is mostly not the case with cats. The personality differences between a Siamese and a Maine Coon aren't noticeable in the same way that, for example, a Jack Russell terrier contrasts with a Great Dane.

It is true that some cat breeds tend to be more vocal, or have other subtle shared traits, but in general most cats act like . . . cats! In fact, if you were to ask cat parents what breed their cat was, most wouldn't know (and many pet cats are mixed breed in any case). They would say something like "She's a tabby." Tabby, by the way, describes a coat color pattern, and is not a breed. In short,

a cat's behavior isn't a function of their breed, but more a product of upbringing, age, and state of health.

Some people are drawn to cats with a certain hair length. Among the long-haired breeds are Persians, Ragdolls, Burmas, Himalayans, Norwegian Forest Cats, Angoras, and Maine Coons. Incidentally, Maine Coons can grow to be over twenty pounds (9 kg)! Shorthaired breeds include Abyssinians, Bobtails, British Shorthairs, Rex, Scottish Folds (with owl-like ears), and Siamese. And, then there's the Sphynx, who is hairless. Keep in mind that a cat with little or no hair has a greater need for warmth because he lacks a fur coat.

053 PICK A PERSONALITY

You may be awestruck by a cat's good looks, but in the end it's probably going to be his personality that wins you over. When choosing the best fit for your family, you'll want to consider your needs. Are you looking for wild and crazy or complacent and lazy? Do you want a kitty who follows you everywhere or do you like the idea of a furry fashion statement who blinks lovingly at you from his perch in the living room? We've all heard pet parents say, "My cat picked me!" or "We were looking at the Siamese, but the orange tabby stuck his paw through the cage and we were sold." That's often how it goes. Depending on whether you get your kitty from a shelter with many cats to choose from or from a local rescue organization or individual with fewer choices, do your best to see past the "look" of a cat and spend some time to learn how you and your prospective new friend feel about one another. Remember, your commitment to your new kitty is for the rest of his life!

054 REFINE YOUR CHOICE

Now that you've polled everyone in the household about longhair versus shorthair (if that matters) and kitten versus adult or senior, it's time to go to the shelter, or to a rescue's adoption event, and meet some cats! Some people just choose the friendliest cat of the bunch, while other people enjoy adopting a timid cat and helping her grow into a more confident character.

Cats, like people can feel under the weather when they are very stressed. If a cat is stressed in a cage at a shelter, she may appear lethargic at that moment, but may turn out to be very energetic and communicative once you get her home and she feels better (and gets to know you). This is very common, so be open to getting to know the cat who may be hiding at the back of the cage or who other adopters may be overlooking!

If you're allowed, and a suitable space is available, let your cat candidate walk around a bit and explore. Does she like being held? If so, do you want a cat that wants cuddles? If you're more accustomed to dogs, you may prefer a more paws-on cat, but if you want a kitty who'll give you space most of the time, that's OK, too. Take your time in choosing. The commitment is for the life of your new buddy, so feel free to fall in love, knowing that you're dedicated to working through any bumps along the way as your feline friend adjusts to you and your home (and vice versa).

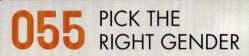

055 PICK THE RIGHT GENDER

They may be a lot smaller, but domestic cats and these huge beauties belong to the same family—Felidae. If you've seen footage of magnificent lions or are lucky enough to have seen them in person in the wild, you may have noticed that some of their behavior is similar to that of your mini-meow. Among other shared traits, large and small kitties like to view the world from a perch, they mark their territory, and they open their mouths to discern particular scents. The head-butt is a sign of affection for felines, and when they're happy, they'll yawn! They all love naps (who doesn't?), and they wiggle their butts when they're about to pounce.

Do you want to adopt a boy cat or a girl cat? Does it matter? Based on our observations of the behavior of thousands of cats, we've found definite patterns based on gender. Aside from the anatomical and chromosomal differences, or maybe partially because of them, we believe there are general behavioral distinctions between boy and girl cats. Of course there are exceptions, and how we socialize kittens and cats makes a huge impact, but here are some patterns we've noticed:

MALE (NEUTERED)	FEMALE (SPAYED)
• Easy-going	• Nurturing
• Adventurous	• Choosy
• Tolerant	• Bossy
• Goofy	• Flirty
• Dependent	• Independent
• Sensitive	• Possessive
• Protective	• Tolerant of boy cats
• Friendly with smaller cats	• Affectionate

056 PROVIDE A TEMPORARY HOME

If you're not sure you can commit to having a cat for years, providing a foster home is a great way to give you some cat time and also help a cat in need. Foster homes are particularly good for cats who are recovering from surgery or illness, or just as a way to free up space in the shelter or give a stressed-out cat a relaxed environment in which to get socialized prior to adoption. Your local rescue group or animal shelter may have a fostering program you can become a part of.

Many foster programs will cover all food and vet costs, and all that is asked of you is to provide care for the cat, and bring the cat to adoption events on weekends. The main difference between adopting and fostering a cat is

that, with fostering, you are only committing yourself to a matter of weeks (usually) and not the whole life of the cat. It's still up to you, though, to create an environment of love, comfort, safety, and nourishment while the cat is a guest in your home.

Also, keep in mind that it can be difficult for you when it's time to say goodbye because that great permanent adopter has come along. In fact, you may have a change in heart about even wanting to find an adopter once you get to know your feline wayfarer, which is OK, too. Although shelters jokingly call these situations "foster failures," the truth is that this isn't a failure at all; if you decide to keep your foster forever, it's a perfect success story.

057 INHERIT A KITTY, HAPPILY

If a family member or someone you know passes away or can no longer care for their cat, and you agree to adopt him, you're doing a wonderful good deed! You and the cat may already have met, which will make things easier. Here are a few things to keep in mind.

BE PATIENT Many cats adapt well to a change of pet parents, but it's important to be patient. Give your new family member lots of love, and make sure he is eating. Lack of appetite is common in this situation because your cat may be feeling the loss of his prior human caretaker, but if he doesn't eat for a couple of days, check in with your veterinarian to avoid missing any serious issues.

UNDERSTAND MOURNING At first, your new kitty may stare out a window or wait by the front door for his original pet parent to arrive. Be careful that he doesn't run outside and become lost! Like a person, your new cat might go through a period of depression. If you are mourning the loss of your friend or family member, too, it's a sweet opportunity for you and the kitty to provide mutual comfort. Given time, you'll both be purring again.

058 FIND A CAT A NEW HOME

If you are in a situation where you have absolutely no alternative but to find your cat a new home (or if you are fostering a cat and need to her find a home), it's vital to make the change as easy as possible for you and your cat. Here are a few ways to find the perfect new pet parent.

PREPARE YOUR CAT Make sure your cat is current with vaccinations and has had a recent vet exam. Naturally, your cat should be spayed or neutered. Never let an unsterilized cat leave your home!

NETWORK & EXPLORE Rather than place an ad in a local paper or online to connect with strangers, begin by networking with friends, family, groups you belong to, and co-workers. Using social media to connect with friends of friends is a good way to go, too. Also, your vets may let you post a flyer in their office. This might lead you to a stranger, but at least it is a stranger who cares enough to take their pets to the vet!

WORK WITH A RESCUE GROUP Some rescue groups allow members of their community who need to rehome a pet to do a courtesy posting on the rescue group's adoption website. If you do this, in return, you'll usually collect an adoption fee from the new pet parent and donate it to the group. As a last resort, if you can't find a

suitable permanent home, you can ask the group if they can take your cat. Rescue organizations are often full to capacity, but offering as large a donation as you can may help them free up resources.

DISCLOSE YOUR KITTY'S FULL BIO Let any prospective parent know everything that's wonderful about your cat, but also reveal any quirks or challenges, including particular interactions with other pets or with children. Make sure prospective new parents understand that your cat is to live a happy and safe life indoors.

EVALUATE A CANDIDATE Always have any prospective pet parent complete an adoption questionnaire (your local rescue group will have these). Read the answers carefully. Does this person seem sincere, stable, and committed to caring for your cat for life? Can you meet this person in a safe place and get to know them a little before handing your cat over? Do they have references, and have they had cats that lived long healthy lives before? Be sure your cat is going to a safe place. If you have any concerns, return any adoption fee and head home with your cat!

FOLLOW UP Don't hesitate to check in by phone or email from time to time. Your cat's new parent may even agree to send you photos of your cat from time to time.

059 DON'T DECLAW!

Declawing a cat is NOT the same as trimming a cat's nails. Trimming cat nails is like trimming your nails. You should do it now and again and, done right, there is no discomfort. Declawing is a surgical procedure that actually amputates the end of the toes and is like removing the ends of your fingers!

There are lots of ways to keep your cat from clawing your furniture—trimming nails is one of the best, and is covered in the CARE section (*see* item 202)—but declawing is not one of them and should NOT be done. It causes pain, comes with medical risks, and leaves a cat without his main weapons should he ever find himself in a situation where he needs his claws to defend himself. Declawing can also change the personality of your cat, causing a once-sweet creature to become aggressive and timid.

060 MEET A CAT ON HER TERMS

Common mistakes people make when petting a kitty for the first time are assuming it's OK to pet a cat's face and head, or, literally, rubbing them the wrong way, in the wrong areas, or in the wrong direction. A cat may run away if a gigantic human stranger, stretches out a tremendous hand towards her face or tries to grab her. Wouldn't you?

OFFER SCENT FIRST Because cats identify people as much by scent as by sight and sound, offering your hand palm down, fingers gently curled under, is a polite way to let a cat get to know your scent. If the cat then rubs your hand with her face, you may take that as a sign to gently pet her head. It's best to do this from behind, rather than bringing your hand directly toward her face. Gently pet her down her neck and partway down the back, moving your hand in the same direction the fur grows.

AWAIT AN INVITATION Let the cat guide you with her body language. If she pushes into you, she's enjoying herself and may want you to pet her more firmly. Avoid petting the tail area until you know her, and never tickle a cat—anywhere. If the cat rolls on her back and seems to offer you her belly, don't fall for it! Touching her there can quickly over-stimulate her, causing her to claw at your hand and even bite as she struggles to get back to her feet and run.

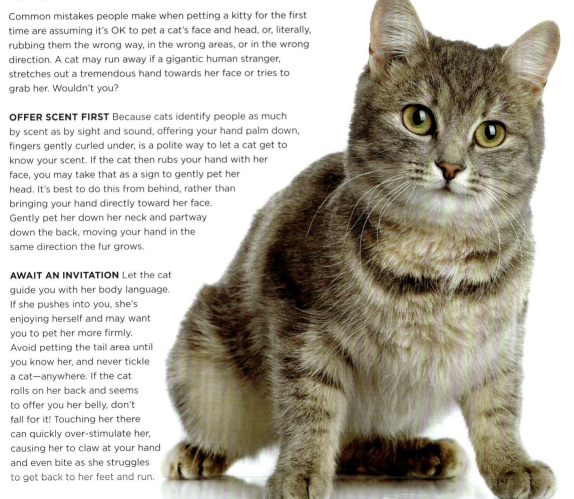

061 TEACH KIDS KITTY 101

So, you recently brought home Manny the Manx. He's settled in, and your children are hoping he's ready to play or snuggle. Until Manny is fully acclimated to your home and everyone in it, ask your children to give him space, and always to be slow and gentle around him.

Kids may lack the strength and coordination to hold a cat in their arms with stability and comfort, so don't encourage them to pick him up until they're old enough and strong enough to handle it, and then only under the careful guidance of an adult. It's also best if they let their new friend come to them instead of heading for him, especially at first. Cats will sometimes approach people if

they're sitting or lying down, but may not be comfortable coming to someone who's standing. Sometimes the hardest lesson for kids is accepting that they may only interact with a cat when the cat is in the mood. Teach them to completely respect their new cat's space.

Here are some reminders that should ensure your kids and the cat get along just fine: Cats tend to default to self-defense ninja moves at the slightest hint of a threat. This could be running and hiding, or it could be scratching or biting. So remind children to always be respectful of their new cat, and remember he does what he wants to do and he is not their toy!

DOS
• Be with your kids when they first meet your new kitty
• Give him space to move away if he wants to
• Be slow and quiet around him
• Let him come to you
• Be respectful of your new friend
• Allow him "down time" in his bed or other sleeping place

DON'TS
• No pulling on your cat's tail or ears
• Be careful not to step on your cat's tail
• No tickles or rough rubs
• No putting your cat in water of any kind
• No picking your kitty up without adult supervision

062 PREPARE THE PET FAMILY

If you already have dogs or cats and are adding a new cat into the mix, that's great! But remember existing pets may be territorial, so bringing home a new cat has to be done in a smart way. Cats in particular do not like changes in their routine, so try to keep things as normal as possible. Be prepared to keep giving lots of love to your existing cat or cats, even as you make time for your new cat as well.

PREPARE A SAFE ROOM If you already have a cat, before bringing in a new cat, prepare a room (perhaps a bathroom or a spare bedroom) where your existing cat doesn't already have a litter box, to be the temporary safe space for your new cat. Be sure there is nowhere in the room for an agile cat to get stuck nor any escape routes. Bring in the new litter box your new cat will use but don't fill it with litter yet. This is so your existing cat can get used to the new object, but won't start using

it. If you don't have a spare room, you can purchase a large multi-tiered cage and place the empty litter box in there. This cage, perhaps partially shrouded by a blanket to afford some privacy for your new cat, can be her temporary home as the two of them slowly and safely become accustomed to one another. Also, be sure to clip the nails of both your existing cat and your new cat prior to introducing them to each other.

KEEP THE DOG OUT If your existing pet is a dog, you will still want that safe room, but you may not want to use a cage since this may just enable your dog to bark at and harass the terrified cat trapped inside. Once the pair have got used to each other and you can allow the cat to roam free, she will become an expert at hiding under a bed or behind a sofa if your dog is showing too much interest. Cats are great at going places where dogs can't follow!

063

INTRODUCE YOUR NEW CAT SLOWLY

When you leave your house to go pick up your new cat from the shelter, close the door to the safe room so there's no chance that your existing cat will be in there when you get home. Close the window too to prevent the newbie escaping—cats can squeeze through the tiniest of gaps.

After you bring your new kitty into the room, shut the door behind you, place the carrier on the floor, and open the carrier's door. Leave it open, as he may want to retreat back in there for a while if he gets nervous. Talk to him soothingly and pet him if he seems to want that. Add the litter to his litter box, and within a half-hour bring him water, along with a tiny bit of dry cat food, bedding, and a toy or two. Spend at least another half-hour with him, and then, when you leave the room, shut the door. For the next several days, when you feed your new cat, place his food dish near the door, and feed your other cat on the other side of the door. When the cats hear simultaneous eating sounds, they'll realize that the other cat is no threat to their food. This is all part of carefully preparing your cats to meet face to face.

064 TAKE IT A STEP FURTHER

Introduce both cats to each other's scents. Bring each cat a blanket the other one has slept on, or a toy the other cat has played with, and them get more familiar with each other's smells. Take turns holding and petting each cat before giving attention to the other. Even if the cats hiss or growl when first detecting each other's scent, they will begin to associate the new smell with you, and this will help them learn the scent is not a threat. Throughout this process, consider giving both cats calming herbal products as directed, or use a pheromone spray in your home. You can find both in any pet supply store.

KEEP IT SHORT After a few days, if you sense things are calm, experiment with holding your new cat wrapped in a towel, then open the door of her room and let her peer into the rest of your house. If she's relaxed, take her for a tour, but be prepared for when your existing and new cats see each other—there may be some commotion. Place your new cat back in the safe room and repeat the tour several times over a day or two. Once the cats have seen each other a few times, you can experiment with leaving the safe room door open while you supervise.

MANAGE THE LITTER BOX During the introductory days, keep the new litter box clean and in the same place. If you intend to move it near the old one, do that over several days by moving it a few feet at a time. You don't want your new cat not to be able to find the box and perhaps relieve herself where it used to be!

Be vigilant about keeping all litter boxes clean, and make sure neither cat ambushes the other while they are trying to use the litter. If the cats get into a scuffle, consider putting your new cat back in the safe room for a day or two until everything calms down.

065

LET YOUR FURRY FRIEND HIDE A WHILE

Don't worry if your new cat mostly hides for a week or so, and only surfaces to eat and use the litter box. Some cats take longer than others to fully integrate into a new household. Likewise, if he is not as affectionate as he was at the shelter or adoption event where you first met him, just give it time. Coming to his forever home is a big adjustment. Don't judge this behavior. Just do all you can to make your new cat feel at home, and your old cat feel loved as well.

066 SPAY OR NEUTER TO SAVE LIVES!

One of the most responsible, important things you can do for your cat is to spay or neuter at the age recommended by your vet. Your life will be easier if you have this done, and your cat will gain numerous significant health benefits as a result. For example, having your female kitty spayed will reduce her risk of getting breast cancer, and it will completely eliminate the threats of uterine and ovarian cancers. Neutering a male cat prevents testicular cancer and prostate problems, as well as hernias and perianal tumors.

FIX BEHAVIORAL ISSUES In both males and female cats, behavioral problems can be eliminated through sterilization. Male cats become less dominant and aggressive, and they'll be much less likely to yowl during the night, since yowling is most often associated with hormonal urges. Neutered males are also much less prone to spraying than unneutered cats. Spayed female cats no longer go into heat, so they won't attract male cats who otherwise may howl and even fight to try to get access to your female kitty.

UNDERSTAND THE NUMBERS Each year millions of cats and dogs are euthanized in the United States due to overpopulation. In most cases, this isn't brought on by homeless pets breeding. It's a problem of too many pets being born, and too few being adopted from shelters. Do your part to ensure your pet does not add to the problem by preventing your cat from creating a litter of kittens. Even if you find homes for all the kittens, those homes are now not available for the kittens and cats that are already in the shelter.

067 GET A CHIP ON YOUR CAT'S SHOULDER

A microchip is a crucial method of identification. It is like a tag, but permanent. The microchip, which is about the size of a grain of rice, is implanted just under the skin between your cat's shoulder blades. It can be detected by a wand-like tool called a scanner and it is an important way that a shelter or veterinarian can identify your cat even if her collar and ID tag have fallen off. Each microchip is assigned a number, which connects to a corresponding record in a microchip database that contains your cat's name, your name, your phone number, your address, and other information. While the chip itself is not a GPS, it will allow someone with a scanner to identify your pet as long as you keep the microchip database updated (this is so important!) with your most current contact information. If you move or change phone numbers, you must remember to update the microchip information! If you don't know how to contact the microchip company to update your information, a shelter or veterinarian can scan your cat and tell you what you need to do.

068 COLLAR YOUR CRITTER

A microchip is a must because it can't fall off, but it does require someone to use a scanner to detect it. So you must also keep a collar and ID tag on your cat so, if your cat gets lost, anyone can immediately read the tag and call you. This saves someone from having to take your cat to a shelter or veterinary office to have him scanned, which many people may not even think to do. A stretch collar is best for your cat; if the collar gets caught on a branch or other object, a stretch collar will give your cat room to breathe and wriggle free without choking. Your ID tag should include the best number to reach you (ideally a cell phone). If there's room, add a second phone number and even your address. If you don't allow your cat outside, you should include a second tag that says "If I am outside, I am lost!" so anyone who finds him will know to call you. Some cats will pull the collar off at first, but if you are patient and keep placing it back on, most cats will eventually get used to it.

069 LET THE COLLAR SHINE

If your cat gets out of your house when it's dark, a reflective collar can make her visible so a passing car is less likely to strike her. A brightly colored collar, such as fluorescent orange, can achieve the same purpose. In fact, in many areas, an orange collar with an ID tag on has come to signify that this is an indoor cat so people will know to return her to you if they find her.

070

LET CATS EAT CAT FOOD

Make a deal with your cat—you won't eat his food and he won't eat yours! Many people don't realize that it's not a good idea to share your table scraps with a cat. Not only is it important for a cat to eat food that is formulated with the right balance of nutrients, but many human foods are toxic to cats. Among them are things we eat tend to eat frequently, such as onions, garlic, and similar root vegetables, along with chocolate, grapes, raisins, tomatoes, avocado, and artificial sweeteners. Additionally, cow's milk can cause diarrhea in cats, so don't think this is a treat for him. While it's possible to find recipes for homemade cat food, virtually all vets recommend pre-made commercial cat food, which you can buy at the pet supply store.

071 HAVE A HAPPY HOLIDAY WITH KITTY

Many a cat has undecorated a decorated Christmas tree, and some have toppled the whole thing, which can be damaging to your house and dangerous for your cat! Additionally, swallowing evergreen tree needles may seriously injure your cat. If you celebrate Christmas and opt for a real tree, consider getting a living tree that comes in a pot of soil. Not only can you plant it out in the garden after the holidays, but when it is properly watered and tended, a living tree won't drop nearly as many needles as a cut one.

072 PROTECT YOUR CAT FROM DECORATIONS

Cats like touching things, and anything smaller than they are, especially if it has movable parts, may very well seem like a toy to them. Hanging ornaments and lights look like a playground to a festive feline. A cat's natural tendency to bat suspended objects is well known. Even worse, tinsel is deadly to cats if ingested.

See how your cat reacts when you put up one or two decorations. If she exhibits no immediate desire to redecorate, put everything else up, but if she is dedicated to attacking your decorations, you may want to find a place for them in your house where she cannot reach them!

BEHAVIOR

> "If animals could speak, the dog would be a blundering outspoken fellow; but the cat would have the rare grace of never saying a word too much."
>
> MARK TWAIN

Cats, rather like people, are motivated by a variety of things, including food, curiosity, and a need to be loved and attended to. It's important to know this, since it will help you to have a great relationship with your own cat and understand a little of why he does what he does. Whether it's chasing and pouncing on a toy, sitting in your lap, or finding a way to open your kitchen cupboard—and then jumping onto a shelf inside it to explore, your cat always has a reason for his behavior. Once you have an insight into his patterns and why he does the things he does, you will be able to reward the good behaviors and steer him away from those you'd prefer he didn't do.

Just as important as understanding why your cat does what he does is noticing when something changes. Changes can be normal as he matures and becomes more relaxed in his environment, but it also can be a sign that something is wrong, or at least not quite right. Cats can't speak with words, but they absolutely do speak with actions and behaviors. Pay attention to your cat, observe his behaviors, and you will begin to understand what he is saying to you.

073

CUDDLE KINDLY

Most cats are fussy about how they're handled. It's best to pick up a cat with two hands, placed just behind her front legs, or with one hand under her abdomen and the other scooping gently behind her hindquarters.

Never pick up your kitty by the tail or legs, or by the neck or collar. This can injure her or freak her out. Be careful and considerate—grab the wrong spot and she'll get upset, scratch and hiss, and may even run away, scared at the prospect of future pick ups!

Keep in mind that not all cats like to be picked up and held, especially by strangers. If your kitty has gotten used to you, that does not mean she'll enjoy being picked up by your friend. Be especially careful when picking up kittens as they can easily squirm out of your hands and fall. They don't always realize how high off the ground they are!

074 APPRECIATE FOOD BURIAL

Imagine you're in a fancy restaurant. You're dressed in nice clothes, sitting across from a good-looking date. The waiter brings out a generous plateful of fine food and you eat most of it. You're full, and sit back in your comfortable chair with a satisfied sigh. And then, you start burying the leftovers with everything in sight: a napkin, your scarf, your date's spare plate, you name it! To cap off the evening, you start to paw at the hard table. Everyone looks at you like you're crazy! To a cat, though, this would seem perfectly normal behavior. Cats engage in the weird ritual of "burying" their leftovers after they've eaten their fill. Sometimes they act like they're covering up the food; at other times, they pretend to paw at the floor. This behavior stems from their strong instinct to hide extra food. In our homes, it serves another important purpose: to make us laugh!

075 UNDERSTAND THE DIRT ROLL

Occasionally, you may see your cat roll around on your floor (or on grass or dirt, if he spends any time outside). If you ever bathe your cat, he may roll even more. This is because, like their feline cousins in the wild, cats like to mask their scent—and this behavior only increases if your cat has a shampoo smell on his skin and hair. Beyond covering up his scent, it may also feel good for your cat to roll around in the dirt! Cats have a lot of nerve endings on their skin, and the ones on their backs get the least amount of stimulation (which is another very good reason for petting and brushing cats). Think of a bear rubbing against a tree to get to an itch on his back: grass, dirt, and even the living room rug make nice scratching surfaces for cats.

076 SAY HELLO TO KITTY

There are many reasons why cats meow. Often it is just your cat saying "hello" and wanting your attention. If you stand in front of your cat and make a meowing sound yourself, you may find that she responds with a meow of her own!

077 LEARN ABOUT REQUESTS

If your cat approaches you and begins to meow in a way that doesn't sound sad, angry, or frightened, but rather inquisitive, he's asking for something. Often, it's his way of asking you when you plan to feed him, or he may want some affection. Or perhaps something is blocking his path to the litter box. It may seem like he's just chatting you up—and he could be—but if he's trying to get your attention, spend a few minutes to see if you can find out what he wants or needs. Keep in mind that a few breeds, such as Siamese, have meows that can sound unhappy. If you listen, you'll get to know why your cat is meowing.

078 NOTICE NEEDS

When kittens mew, as they do frequently, it may be a greeting, but it's more likely out of need: they're asking for food, or they're scared, in pain, or uncomfortable in some other way. They may be cold, for example. If a kitten is eight weeks old or younger, her mews are like the cries of a baby. They are your kitten's attempts to get you to help out with one of the things that her mom would usually provide.

079 JOIN IN THE CHATTER

Is your cat intently staring out the window at a bird on a branch and "chattering" in a kind of shaky, high-pitched, breathy way? If so, she is expressing excitement at what she's observing (or maybe the desire to attack what she sees as prey). Your feline hunter has deep-rooted instincts akin to those of wild cats, and this chatter is proof of that. It's a harmless noise, but it should remind you that cats need plenty of stimulation, so be sure your cat can exercise her in-built desire to chase and pounce when you play with her.

080 LISTEN TO YOWLS

Some cats are very vocal when they're hungry. Especially with a new cat, it is important to find out why your cat is vocalizing. If it sounds like he's pleading or complaining, then he's probably unhappy, and you need to do something about it.

For example, if your cat lets out loud, long howls or yowls, he's likely in some kind of distress. If you can see that he's not faced with any obvious physical dilemma—he's not stuck somewhere or threatened by something or someone—he may be in pain due to an illness or injury. Try to discover the source of his discomfort, and if it's not something you can identify and remedy yourself, take him to the vet immediately.

We highly recommend you spay or neuter your cat. But if your female cat isn't yet spayed, this kind of crying may mean she's in heat. Otherwise, your cat (whether male or female) may be howling because another animal is nearby and your cat feels challenged or threatened. If there is an unneutered male cat in the vicinity, his scent may incite a lot of vocalization from your cat.

081 INTERPRET GROWLS

If your is cat growling, beware! He is sending out a strong warning that an explosion of anger is about to happen! Just as with a dog, respect the growl and back off. However, if your cat is growling at another pet in your home, step between them and break up the problem before it turns into a scuffle.

082 TEACH YOUR KITTY KEY PHRASES

If you spend hours on end with your cat, chances are you'll talk to her from time to time. And weirdly enough, it might even start to seem as if she understands what you're saying. That is because she does! Just like dogs, cats can understand words and associate them with actions. Here are some strategies to adopt.

REPETITION To teach your cat key phrases, repetition is vital. Saying "Time to eat," "Let's go to sleep," or "No jumping on the counter" will start to make sense to your cat when you say it the same way and in the same circumstance again and again.

TONE OF VOICE Try using the same tone of voice, and emphasizing the same words, each time you utter these phrases. If your cat is being the perfect angel, try speaking to her in a higher-pitched voice to encourage that behavior. Likewise, lowering your tone or adding a hard edge to it conveys disapproval. A hissing sound is a good way to say "No" to a cat. The more you talk to her, the better your cat will become at understanding what you are saying.

083 LEARN HOW CATS PURR

Cats may start purring as soon as a couple of days after birth, possibly as a way to bond with their moms. Purring begins when your cat's brain sends messages to his throat muscles, making them twitch at a dizzying rate of 25 to 150 vibrations in a single second. This vibration makes your cat's vocal cords separate as he breathes in and out, and presto: the purr! Some cats purr so vigorously that they drool at the same time.

But what does purring mean? Usually a purr signals contentment, and that is how most people understand it. Cats may also purr to let you know they need something. Also, a purr can be a self-soothing technique for the cat.

084 DISCOVER WHY CATS KNEAD

Kneading is a rhythmic alternate pressing of paws against a soft object and is among the cutest and most curious things cats do. It is often accompanied by purring. Like purring, kneading begins shortly after birth—when kittens knead their paws against their mother to stimulate milk production. Kneading can also reflect your kitty's quest to fluff up a surface to make it soft and comfortable before she takes a nap. Sometimes your cat will knead while happily stretching. If you're petting a cat who's curled up in your lap, and she starts kneading you, chances are she's feeling very relaxed. To stay comfortable (and to avoid your clothes getting tattered), be sure to keep your cat's nails trimmed (*see* item 202) if she's a regular kneader!

GRUMPY CAT

Some celebrities are born, not made, and this is the case with Tardar Sauce, now much better known as "Grumpy Cat." Tardar Sauce gained notoriety when her photograph was posted on Reddit in 2012. Many people found her unusual expression sweet and funny and so they shared the photograph, making her widely famous.

BIRTH NAME
Tardar Sauce

STAGE NAME
Grumpy Cat

BORN
April 4, 2012, in Morristown, Arizona

YOU TUBE HITS
19 million and counting

FILMS
Lil Bub and Friendz (2013)
Grumpy Cat's Worst Christmas Ever (2014)

TRIVIA
BuzzFeed's "Meme of the Year" 2013

The "face" of "Grumppucino" line of coffee drinks.

Merchandise includes mugs, T-shirts, and stuffed toys

Tardar lives with Tabatha Bundesen, who has explained that the cat's facial expression is caused by a form of dwarfism, which has given her an underbite. Her mother was a normal cat, but her father is not known.

When it became clear that Tardar had become a celebrity, Tabatha took time off work to manage her schedule. Tabatha's brother Bryan looks after the Grumpy Cat website, Facebook, YouTube, and Twitter accounts, while Ben Lashes is her publicist.

Grumpy Cat has been featured on the front page of *The Wall Street Journal* (May 30, 2013) and on the cover of *New York* magazine (October 7, 2013). She is to get her own animatronic waxwork at Madame Tussauds in San Francisco, while her many celebrity appearances include *Today, Good Morning America,* CBS *Evening News, Anderson Live, Big Morning Buzz Live, The Soup,* and *American Idol.* At heart, though, she's just a simple kitty!

085

DESCRIBE A CAT FACE

You would know your own cat anywhere, but could you describe her to a stranger? Start with her face: cute little nose, green eyes, pointy ears—that could be almost any cat. Look again. You may think that cats are much the same except, perhaps, for their color, but once you start looking, you'll notice that their appearance can vary quite a lot. For example, there are at least three distinct cat head and face shapes and many variations in between. See if you can find your cat's face shape among the types shown here.

ROUND FACE

American, European, and British Shorthairs are good examples of breeds with this appealing, well-balanced face.

FLAT FACE

Probably the best known flat-face cat is the Persian. This face shape can cause breathing and eating problems, along with runny eyes.

POINTED FACE

Long, pointed faces tend to go with a slim and slinky body type (see item 127) and often belong to Siamese and Oriental breeds.

086 SURRENDER YOUR SWEATER

OK. You're minding your own business, maybe watching TV, and your cat emerges from your bedroom with your favorite sweater in her mouth. She's sucking the thread, and seems to be enjoying every morsel. So much for wearing that pretty sweater to work tomorrow!

Sucking on woolly fibers may be a carryover from her nursing days and is probably comforting to your cat. Sucking on your sweater, shoelaces, and fuzzy hats (along with anything else she can find) may mean she was separated from her mother too early or that she's experiencing separation anxiety or other stress right now—hence the kitten-like behavior.

To keep your sweaters safe, aside from storing them out of reach on a high shelf, you can give your cat a soft toy instead (or you can always gift her that ugly sweater your thoughtful aunt got you for Christmas!).

087 WATCH FOR PAIN

Cats can be proud creatures, and sometimes that means they put on a brave face when they are in pain. Unlike dogs, which live in packs, cats live solitary lives in the wild, so they don't tend to cry out for help, or otherwise draw attention to themselves, as this can alert a predator that they are hurt—and vulnerable. Your cat still has this instinct despite your eagerness to take care of him.

To pinpoint pain, look out for changes in your cat's behavior: is he hiding away more than usual, or laying in an odd spot in your house? Is he refusing to eat food, or drinking water at odd times? If anything's unusual, it's better to be safe than sorry—take your precious pet to the vet. If you wait until the pain is obvious, your cat may be really suffering, and the situation could become very serious, or even life-threatening.

088 ACCEPT IT: THEY'RE MIND READERS

If you've ever lived with a cat for a while, you've likely been struck by how spookily astute they can be. They can pick up on your moods, such as appearing in bed to offer a reassuring snuggle the very instant you wake up from a bad dream. Or perhaps you've had a cat follow you into the kitchen, seeming to know when you're about to feed her. Maybe you've even noticed your cat sit by the door ten minutes before your husband or wife walks through it! So . . . are you living with a small, furry psychic?

The truth is arguably more impressive. Cats' astounding "telepathy" likely stems from their super-powered senses. Their ears can distinguish sounds three times higher than humans. Their sight is also more impressive than ours, detecting movement far more sharply (although they don't see colors so well). In their tiny noses, cats have twice as many scent receptors than humans do. They even have a scent-detecting organ in the roof of their mouth.

Cats are also ultra-aware of our body language, to the point where they seem to be able to tell we're angry, scared, upset, content, or bored even before we know it ourselves. If you're about to take your cat to the veterinarian and she runs and hides right on cue, it's most probably because she has picked up on a spectrum of nonverbal signals that you didn't even know you were emitting, and is acting accordingly.

With their heightened senses and amazing awareness of body language, cats act like the ultimate mind readers, ensuring you won't be able to hide a thing!

EXTRAORDINARY HEARING

AWESOME EYESIGHT

INCREDIBLE SENSE OF SMELL

089 COPE WITH FOOD REFUSAL

Sudden loss of appetite is a sign that something may be wrong with your cat. Ignoring grub he used to gobble down could mean he is battling an ailment. But don't panic right away: in cat land, not wanting to eat a meal can be symptomatic of a host of other issues.

To find out what's going on, first offer an alternative. It may be that the food you were giving had somehow spoiled or he just doesn't feel like it today. Second, consider outside influences. Changes to his environment could cause your kitty to refuse food: did someone new recently move in or come to visit? Anxiety may be to blame—if your cat recently had a scary scuffle with

another cat, for example. Strategies for whetting his appetite include offering him a smidgen of canned tuna or cooked liver. If after a day or two, your kitty's still not eating his food, take him to the vet.

090 GIVE KITTY WHAT SHE WANTS

Face it—your feline friend likes her space. This doesn't mean she doesn't relish every moment you spend together. It's just a fact of being a cat that she likes to be some distance from moving objects when she's not engaged in play, and she needs her beauty sleep.

KITTY NEEDS ROOM In order to feel content and relaxed so that they can thrive in your home, cats need assurance that they are physically safe. However, although they like hugs and games, most don't need to be touched or played with as much as dogs do. Cats are protective of their bodies and take their personal space very seriously, so we humans need to respect it.

KITTY NEEDS COMPANY If only that respect was mutual! When they're feeling social, or needy, or just plain impish, cats throw all space considerations aside. They will quite happily pounce on your toes while you're trying to sleep, or sit at the edge of the tub meowing while you're trying to take a relaxing bath.

091 BOOST CAT CONFIDENCE

Cats' personalities can vary nearly as much as ours do. Some kitties are true social butterflies, while others prefer to be demure wallflowers. If your cat falls into the latter category, you may wish to coax him to be a little more confident.

Some cats take timidity to the extreme and are embodiments of scaredy-cats. They get spooked by loud noises, run and hide when any stranger is around, and seem truly distressed at even the most innocuous sudden movement. Sometimes this reactivity is written in their DNA, but it can also be the result of a traumatic time in their lives when they felt less than safe.

Giving your scaredy-cat confidence takes patience and time. It's crucial that timid felines get the space they need, so they can trust that their human will not enter their comfort zone or make them leave it. If a timid cat approaches you, offer kisses and cuddles, but don't force it. Remain calm and quiet around a skittish cat, and do your best not to make sudden movements or loud noises. Kneel down, if you can, and play with him at his level. Over time, your cat will come to realize that you aren't a source of anxiety, but rather one of gentle, non-threatening stability. Then his confidence in you—and eventually in his now-secure position in life—will definitely blossom.

092 AVOID AGGRESSION TRIGGERS

Cats are wonderful family members, but it's important to remember that they're also animals with strong instincts. One of these instincts is to use their powerful built-in weapons (teeth and claws—yikes!) when they are hunting or to defend themselves if they feel threatened. The key in avoiding or at least reducing aggression is to understand what kinds of activities or behaviors may trigger biting or scratching, and don't go there!

TRESPASSING

Cats can be territorial. Say you bring a new cat to meet your existing cat in your home. She may perceive this as a threat to her territory and may crouch (a defensively aggressive move), or lash out at the intruder. She may resort to hissing, biting, swatting, or chasing. Dogs, other small animals, or even unfamiliar humans can all make your kitty feel her territory is under attack.

PLAYING

When you roughhouse with your cat, you're risking that she will take it a step too far. Remember, even though they are tiny, those claws and teeth are very sharp and can cut deeply! Even if the cat's intentions aren't bad, unguarded playing can bring on "play aggression," which risks doing real damage to you. Play gently and stop if it looks like your cat is getting overexcited.

PETTING

Gentle petting usually feels good to a cat, and she lets you know by purring or looking relaxed. But just occasionally, between strokes, she'll nip or lightly bite the petter and then rush away. Perhaps you touched a sensitive spot or were too aggressive in your petting. Keep an eye on how she's reacting and always touch her slowly and gently. Stop if she looks unhappy.

HUNTING

Say, your cat is sitting at the window watching a couple of birds batting their wings. This gets your kitty all riled up. But she can't reach the birds, so she turns to you and lashes out. She is frustrated and just can't control herself. Being unable to reach the object of her attention is a common cause of "redirected aggression," which can cause your placid cat to go a little nuts.

093 PLAY NICE!

Although it might be tempting to treat your cat like a young child and include exciting games in your play, such as pretend-wrestling or lifting him up and giving him the feeling he is flying, resist! Chances are, he's more fragile than you think, and your play session may end with some painful scratches for you.

Your cat may interpret roughhousing as a threat and subsequently become afraid of you, putting a damper on your relationship until you regain his trust. And, of course, if your cat is afraid enough, biting and scratching can follow. Rough play can also risk damaging your feline friend's dainty bones. As fun as it might be to act out a wrestling match with your little companion, ultimately it's better to be safe than sorry. "Handle with care" is an appropriate mantra when playing with cats.

094

BE ALERT TO ALPHA BEHAVIOR

When you have more than one cat, they might challenge each other to determine who's boss, especially if one cat is trying to assert his or her dominance.

SEE WHO'S BOSS Asserting dominance is known as alpha behavior, named after the head of a pack of wolves (the jury's still out on whether or not cats have a true pack hierarchy). When you feed multiple cats, for example, the alpha cat will likely eat first while the others wait their turn. A dominant cat may steal a toy from another cat, or even swat him on the face, just to remind him who's in charge.

WATCH FOR ROLE REVERSAL You might notice the alpha role alternates among cats in a multi-cat home. One cat might be the alpha when it comes to eating, while another may dominate the sleeping arrangements, sprawling over the bed as the other stays on the floor. Roles can change if one cat dies, a new cat enters the family, or if you move to a new home where the alpha cat feels less secure.

STAY ON TOP OF THE HEAP You may sometimes feel like an alpha cat is bullying you: nipping at your nose to get you out of bed in the morning, or growling if you approach him when he is eating. When you pet him too vigorously, he can become irritated and lash out. An alpha cat can be something of a handful! The main thing to watch for is that he does not become so dominant as to make another cat in your household feel perpetually unsafe. If this occurs, you need to intervene to give love and support to the meek cat and let the alpha cat know when he is crossing the line from alpha to bully.

095

LET KITTY BE KING (OR QUEEN)

What should you do when one of your cats really begins to bully another cat?

As tempting as it may be to scold Queen Alpha, try to resist as long as she is not harming the other cat with her bossy ways. Scolding can make matters worse. Remember that she isn't being malicious, she's just stepping up to fulfill an important role within the group. It doesn't hurt to let your dominant cat rule—after all, it's part of her personality and may have been a survival trait at some point in her life.

While letting your alpha cat reign in her cat kingdom, you should also look after the non-alpha kitties, and make sure that they are not harmed in any way by their more dominant friend. Give all your cats the emotional security and attention that they need, and if the alpha interrupts your snuggle time with another cat, gently shoo the alpha away. Also don't let her bully you; if she persistently nips you in the morning, for instance, insist she stay outside your bedroom with the door firmly closed between you. Try to make things as equitable as possible so every cat in your house knows they are loved and protected.

096 BREAK UP A BRAWL!

If you have more than one cat in your home, you'll know that cats don't always get along. Just like human siblings, they can have their quarrels—and with cats those quarrels can become real scuffles. Even if you only have one cat, he might get into a conflict with another cat in the neighborhood. The good news is that it's extremely rare for disagreements to escalate to the point where they are out of control, or where they cause serious harm to the cats that are involved.

To prevent cat fights from occurring, it helps to know a bit about why they start in the first place. Remember that cats, like dogs, can be hierarchical in their social circles (see item 094). Rather than being all relaxed about other cats entering their space, they are hyper-aware of their

territory and often guard it fiercely! So if one of your cats is used to ruling the roost in your living room, he probably won't be all that thrilled the minute a newly adopted second cat moseys in.

If your cats are staring each other down in a true confrontation, make a loud hissing sound or even stomp the ground with your foot. This will distract them and will likely cause them both to bolt in different directions, ending the confrontation. If your cats are in the middle of a swatting fight, again make lots of noise but don't be tempted to intervene with your hands or you may be deeply scratched or bitten. Tussles like that are usually very quickly over and the cats will disengage as soon as one can run away.

FACT OR FICTION?

A CAT THAT SCRATCHES IS MEAN

Cats sometimes do scratch, but that doesn't make them mean. Typically they scratch due to fear (often when cornered) or overstimulation (perhaps from a belly rub). If your cat's an angel with everyone but your loud uncle, it could be that she fears him. The same goes for a child who may not know how to properly handle your kitty, or is scared of her. Your cat may associate interaction with danger, since she can sense that the child is afraid. An unneutered or recently adopted cat may also scratch at first. It's important to treat a cat carefully for some time after spaying or neutering to give your cat a chance to become more hormonally balanced.

097 APPLAUD THE POUNCE

Ever notice how cats can go from sleepy to feisty in less than a split second? Jungle cats, such as tigers, need to be ready to move at a moment's notice. Safely sprawled in your living room, your pet may not have to perform this kind of sudden hunting behavior—but often she'll go for it anyway and pounce!

The average cat is quick to pounce on moving objects. Say you are knitting with your cat curled up on your lap. You drop the ball of yarn, and in the blink of an eye she's leaping out of your lap and running after that yarn at lightning speed. She catches it and pounces on it, grasping it between sharp claws.

Enjoy the show as your little tiger plays out her fantasy of being the queen of the jungle and when the game is finished, remember to put the yarn out of reach so she can't eat it, which can be harmful.

098 ACCEPT KITTY'S INNER LION

Like a fierce lion, your sweet-looking kitty has a predatory side. Hunting and chasing come naturally to him. Smaller animals like rabbits may be able to run faster than a cat, but he makes up for it by sneaking up on his prey and then pouncing with the type of aggression that reminds you of his mighty cousin.

But it's more than predatory prowess that links our family cats with lions. Lions like to rub up against things. This slinky move is mostly about marking territory. While your cat rubs up against your leg to reinforce that you belong to him, his wild cousin may press his body against a big tree to say, "This is mine."

Both lions and domesticated cats have a playful side; get two lions together and they sometimes butt heads gently, just like two domesticated cat friends do. Lions and kitty-cats alike relish a nice, high perch from which they can regally survey their surroundings. And both species love to groom, giving themselves elaborate tongue baths. They share a great sense of smell, enhanced when they open their mouths, where they have a special gland that picks up more scent. And the list goes on—with one big difference: as fierce as he fancies himself to be, your kitty wouldn't last a day in the jungle.

099 MANAGE KITTY'S VERMIN FASCINATION

One of the most alarming aspects of life with a cat is the "gifts" of mice, or other small animals she may catch and bring to you—dead or alive, or somewhere in between! Disgusting and disagreeable as this may be, try to see it from your cat's perspective. Hunting, pouncing on, and finishing off the real or imagined vermin she sees around her is deeply ingrained in a cats' genetic code. And by bringing the small animal to you, your cat is showing off.

If you keep any rodents as pets, protect them from your cat's dangerous claws. Don't underestimate your cat's tenacity as a hunter; keep your hamster or pet mouse securely out of kitty's reach—preferably up high, and definitely in a secure cage or crate! Even if your cat can't actually get at your little critter, she can still terrorize him, so ensure this is not going to happen—your tiny pet has a right to a safe and happy life, too!

ENCLOSE Set up an outdoor enclosure in your yard for your cat, preventing him from reaching birds while still allowing him to bask in the sun (*see* item 205).

ALARM Attach a bell to his collar. That way, birds are warned of his presence and know to stay clear.

CLIP Trim your cat's nails, curtailing his ability to climb in pursuit of prey (*see* item 202).

100
PROTECT WILD BIRDS

If you look out into the trees of your backyard you may see all manner of birdlife. Well, your cat sees just one thing: prey! It is virtually impossible to deter your cat from pursuing birds, and if he catches one—often by sneaking up from behind, or climbing a tree—instinct will kick in and he'll kill it. Take the steps here to reduce his hunting prowess, and keep the birds a little safer.

101 SHIELD PET BIRDS

If you have a rescued parrot or other pet bird, make sure you do not leave your cat in its vicinity unattended. The bird's living area, whether it's a cage or a crate, should be way up high; you'd be surprised how far your cat can leap off the floor, or jump from a nearby piece of furniture, when he's dead set on pursuit. If he likes to lurk around the base of the birdcage, you can make that area less appealing by drenching it in your kitty's least favorite smells: citrus is a good deterrent, and there are some sprays on the market designed to discourage cats.

102 TAKE CARE OF CLAWING

Cats' claws are sharp! Whether the target is that brand new couch or your skin, the damage they cause can be painful, extensive, and expensive.

KNOW WHY First and most importantly, cats scratch because it feels good. It works off energy, makes for a satisfying stretch, and helps them remove the dead outer layer of their claws. They also scratch to mark their territory: paws contain sweat glands, leaving behind an odor to go with those unsightly scratch marks.

USE DETERRENTS If your cat's scratching is becoming a problem for you, try some safe deterrents. The first is simply to keep your cat's nails trimmed, or apply nail caps (see item 025). Sticking double-sided tape on your furniture where your cat is scratching can also help because the stickiness on her paws will annoy her and put her off doing it again. You can also try placing covers over the objects or furniture you most want to protect. Spraying cat-deterring scents in selected areas can also be very effective (see item 024).

DIVERT ATTENTION A good way to discourage your cat from clawing at that pristine sofa is to place scratching pads right near it. These pads, which come in a range of shapes, are ideal distractions. There are plenty of other objects you can employ as outlets for your cat's claws. A trip to the pet store will yield toys of all shapes and sizes, but even a cardboard box or a simple log can make a great toy for a scratch-happy cat!

103 REWARD GOOD BEHAVIOR

Beyond being a wonderful bonding experience for the two of you, positive reinforcement is a highly effective training method. Many of us love our feline family members and want to shower them with praise, treats, petting, and kisses 24/7, but praise and the occasional treat can also be used to teach your kitty that what he just did is exactly what you want him to do. Like babies, cats have short attention spans. It's important to reward their good behavior immediately after it occurs. If your cat uses the litter box and you want to reward him, throw a treat his way just as he's finishing up so he knows what the reward is for. Use verbal praise as well, so your kitty doesn't gain weight from too many treats.

104 DON'T TOY WITH TRUST

Despite the preponderance of online videos where dogs are taunted with pieces of sausage on their noses that they can't eat, or where owners throw "toys" that aren't really there, the fake-out is a lousy trick to play on a pet (or a human), so don't do it. If you hint to your cat that you're about to reward him with a treat, or snuggles, or access someplace he'd like to go, and then you don't follow through, you're teaching him not to trust you. If you offer something nice, deliver on your promise. Animals learn patterns of behavior. So if you're inconsistent in your verbal communication and body language, you'll wind up confusing your pet.

105 ADDRESS PROBLEM BEHAVIOR

Cats are great housemates and most of the time we love having them around, but sometimes they can be irritating ("helping" with the cooking) or they may do something downright dangerous (such as knocking over a candle). Cats are great jumpers and your kitty can easily leap up onto your fireplace mantel, dining room table, or kitchen counters. Remember, she won't have a clue that what she is doing is unacceptable unless you let her know. Gently lifting her off the candlelit table or the kitchen counter while saying simple words such as "No" or "Get down" in a firm tone will help her understand that you don't like that behavior. If your hands are full or you can't reach your cat just as something bad is about to happen, you can even make a loud hissing sound—she will understand this as extreme displeasure and, hopefully, she'll jump away from the dangerous situation.

Occasionally, something you do may inadvertently trigger an aggressive or fearful reaction in your cat. If you bring a new cat into the home, for example, your old cat may hide and refuse to come out or even start to spray the furniture with urine to mark territory. It's annoying, but you should remember that it's also a cat's natural response to feeling threatened by what she sees as an intruder. Remove or avoid bad-behavior triggers (*see* item 092) and always introduce new cats slowly (*see* item 063). Finally, look out for and reward good behavior with treats and praise to turn your devilish little kitty into a perfect angel!

106 CRACK KITTY'S CODES

Sometimes it seems that cats enjoy confusing us, but they're more likely trying to communicate with body language. Here is a cheat sheet to help you decipher a few common kitty-cat codes. Keep your eyes open!

A SLOW-MOVING TAIL

Your cat is calm and relaxed.

A PLAINTIVE MEW

Your cat is hungry for attention or food.

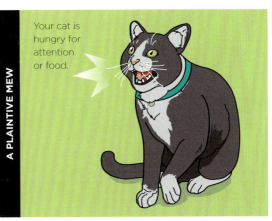

A WILDLY WHIPPING TAIL

Your cat is primed for action and adventure.

A SLOW BLINK

Your cat is content, loved, and loving.

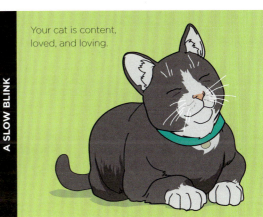

A YAWN

Your cat is feeling mellow.

KNEADING WITH PAWS

Your cat is very happy!

107 DECIPHER FULL-BODY LANGUAGE

Cats are geniuses at making their intentions and desires known, but you have to speak their language! Besides the meow, they utilize many other modes of communication. They often demonstrate their feelings with their entire bodies, such as when they roll around on their backs (to show contentment or invite petting) or when they rub up against a standing human's legs (a sign of affection or possibly a flirty request for food or attention).

108 SEE INTO THESE EYES

As with humans, the pupils in a cat's eyes naturally dilate (enlarge) in the dark to allow in more light and, of course, they shrink when the cat is in a bright area. But, if your cat's pupils are dilated and she hasn't recently been in the dark, it means she's stimulated and trying to gather more information about her surroundings. She may be feeling excitement, aggression, anxiety, or even pain. If her pupils remain dilated, it could be a sign of a health problem, so have her checked out by a vet.

If your kitty's pupils suddenly constrict, and it doesn't seem to be because of a change in light, she could be angry, or she may be ready to pounce on something.

109 FOLLOW THE EARS

When your cat's ears are positioned straight upward, she is probably content—or at least unbothered. If she's walking and her tail is also upright, she's relaxed and happy. When her ears shift to the side, it's in reaction to sound. If she wants to identify the sound, she'll probably turn her head toward it. If she's irritated by it, the ear shift is intended to try to muffle the sound. When a cat's ears lie flat backwards, she's ready for a fight or a pounce!

110 TELL TALES

A cat's tail can express mood and it also serves as a medium to notify you about what may happen next. The slow, back and forth moving tail is a sign of contentment. You may notice your kitty does this once in a while, especially when eating.

When your cat's tail is pointing straight upward, she's a happy pussycat, so long as the fur on the tail lies flat. If her tail is erect and the fur is bushy, she may be scared or angry. If she's in motion and her tail is down (or between her legs), she's nervous; she may also creep across the floor with her body close to the ground. She's trying to make herself as small as possible by literally keeping a low profile, in response to a perceived danger. If her tail is out straight behind her as she walks, she may be fine—not overly happy, but not necessarily unhappy. If you observe this, try cheerfully talking to her. Chances are, if everything's OK, her tail will shoot upwards.

If she's flicking her tail back and forth rapidly, she's stimulated. This may be a playful sign, if she's about to pounce on something fun, but it can also signify aggression and agitation. If she is clearly not playing, and you can see other signs of anger or annoyance, such as sharply narrowed or very enlarged eye pupils, laid-back ears, and especially if you hear a growl, she may be about to get into a scuffle with one of your other pets!

111
PAY ATTENTION TO PANTING

It is unusual to see a cat pant. It usually means they are very stressed. For example, your cat may howl and then pant when you are transporting him in his carrier to the vet's office for a checkup. Cats also sometimes open their mouths and look like they are panting, but they are actually using an organ in the top of his mouth that increases their sense of smell, so they may be stalking a rodent or otherwise trying to better track a scent. If it is a warm day and your cat has been vigorously playing, he may pant to cool off like a dog. If you see your cat panting and there is no obvious reason, take him to the vet for a checkup because he may be in pain.

112 HELP DOGS AND CATS BE FRIENDS

We know that cats often face-off among each other to determine status, and that they hunt and lunge after birds and rodents like it's their job. But how do cats view dogs? Because cats and dogs often appear like night and day, people sometimes assume they won't get along. But that's not true. In fact, they can be best friends.

While both cats and dogs can be territorial, cats generally focus more on protecting their space, while dogs focus on the people or other animals with whom they're trying to bond. A cat may, therefore, interpret a dog's playful advances as a threat to her personal space.

So, to avoid an encounter that could sour the relationship, take things slowly. When introducing a cat to a dog, to begin with keep the cat safely behind a door where some sniffing can be done, but touching cannot. The next step is to show the dog and cat to each other, but with the cat in a crate and the dog on a leash. This will make physical contact impossible until both creatures get more comfortable with each other. Don't place your cat, even in a carrier, on the ground where a dog can make her feel threatened. With care, after a short amount of time, cats and dogs can become close, sometimes even inseparable.

113 PAUSE THE PAPERWORK

A surefire way to get your cat's full attention is to try to settle down and read a newspaper (or work on a computer or even read a book)! You may find your cat just has to plop down right on top of whatever you are reading. Beyond the warmth and comfort she's getting from your lap—if that is where she has landed— she's also making a play for your attention. She sees the focus you're giving your papers, maybe even turning the pages and writing on them, and she wants it for herself!

114 WALK YOUR CAT (MAYBE)

Have you ever seen someone walking a pet cat down the street? Such a sight is rare. Walking a cat is possible, but most cats have no interest in taking this sort of exercise. Unlike their canine buddies, cats prefer to remain out of sight, and want to be free to run and jump out of harm's way if necessary. If you have an extremely confident cat that is not fearful in any way, you might find she enjoys a little time on a leash in your front yard.

You'll first need the right gear. Use a chest harness. (A leash and collar can be dangerous; if your cat escapes and runs up a tree, this setup could strangle her.) Trial and error may be necessary until you find a harness your cat likes (or tolerates), one that can be adjusted to fit securely. A vest-style harness is good since it will be more difficult for a resistant, resourceful cat to wiggle her way out of. Vet harnesses are also probably most comfortable for your kitty. Adjust the harness so it's tight enough to stay on, but not so tight that she will feel restricted. Fit the harness and try it out indoors before venturing outside.

115 MAKE A NEW START

When you adopt a cat, you may not know the details of her background. She may have come from a happy home, where she was cuddled and coddled at every opportunity, and then her owner passed away or could no longer continue to care for her. But the stress of being dropped off at an animal shelter or being moved between foster homes may have made her a bit nervous, and even frightened of her new surroundings.

The good news is that as her new owner, you have a chance to give her the fresh start she deserves. It's OK not to know every little detail about your cat's past. Her new life with you begins today! Now is your chance to develop new routines and traditions, to test the waters in your new relationship, and forge a long-term bond.

Be sure you don't rush it and expect to become instant friends. Just as with people, it might take a little time for you both to get comfortable together and to learn each other's likes and dislikes. Your new cat may need time to heal from a hardship (physical or emotional) she's had in the past. So plan on taking some time to get to know her needs and preferences as you carve out your life together.

116 ESTABLISH TRUST GRADUALLY

When you bring your new cat home—from a shelter or anywhere else—understand that he'll need at least twenty-four hours simply to adjust to the shock of brand-new surroundings, and it may take days or weeks for him to really feel comfortable. Remember, he may be confused as to why he is in a new home with all these new smells, people, and even other pets. Don't expect him to jump into your arms like he has lived with you for years. He doesn't know that you are trustworthy and mean him no harm. Cats are sensitive souls, and like anyone else, they need some time to adjust to their new environment. And, when a cat has been through any sort of upheaval, reestablishing trust is a process that requires patience—sometimes a lot of patience.

117 TAKE IT SLOW

Resist the temptation to rush over to your new cat and scoop her up and kiss her all over! There will be time for that in the future. For now, be patient and let her take the lead on how much touching and cuddling she wants. Pacing yourself and tuning in to her cues will pay off as she learns to trust you.

118 GET ON HIS LEVEL

When approaching your new feline family member—whether in a small enclosed space like a bathroom or in a larger area once you allow him to roam your house—crouch down slowly and begin to gently pet him if he will come to you. Never corner him or force yourself on him, and don't pet him too vigorously. Vigorous petting, and especially touching his stomach, can overstimulate him, and he might react by running away or suddenly clawing or biting you.

119 KEEP IT SIMPLE

Be strategic with your touch when your cat first starts accepting you as a friend. Avoiding her tail, face, and stomach is smart, as too much contact with these areas can put a cat on guard. Even if she seems like she wants her tummy rubbed, think twice, as this is an area that cats do guard fiercely. Start by rubbing the back of her head gently, working down to a light, comforting stroke of her back if she seems to be relaxed and enjoying herself.

Although it may seem counterintuitive, resist making direct eye contact with your new cat, and if you do look into her eyes, don't do it for too long. Cats can see this as an aggressive gesture, so it might make her ill at ease.

120 PICK THE MOMENT

If and when he seems amenable to it, try picking up your cat and and holding him gently against your chest for just a moment and then placing him back down. That way he will learn that letting you pick him up is not a bad thing and that he will soon be returned to the ground. It is important he learns to trust you because you may need to pick him up and place him in a carrier for a vet visit or in an emergency evacuation from your home. After a while, you should detect behavior that reveals your less-is-more approach is working. Your cat may start to come to you and tell you he wants more loving by rubbing up against you or purring.

121 MAKE A CAT-SAFE FENCE FOR YOUR OUTDOOR KITTY

While your cat craves the great outdoors, you may fret about feisty fellow felines, roaming raccoons, deer ticks, diseases, and poor drivers every time he sets paw in the backyard. Happily, if you already have a fence around your property, you can keep him enclosed—and outside dangers at bay. Plug any holes in the fence, then add a barrier around the top. Various kits are available. Alternately, if you have a deck or patio, you can erect a "roof" over the top (*see* item 205). Remember to provide a litter box and toys to entertain kitty.

1 YOU NEED Buy brackets (hinged is an option), mesh, and fixings.

2 FIX SUPPORT Attach the brackets to the top of the fence at every fence post.

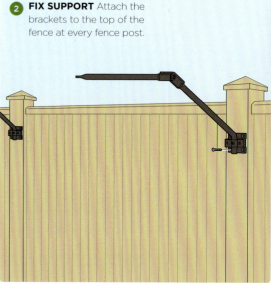

3 ADD MESH Use cable ties to fasten the mesh in place on the brackets.

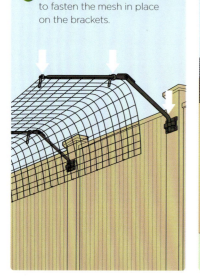

4 AT THE GATE Fix one bracket near the hinges and one on the gate. The mesh will fold back when the gate opens.

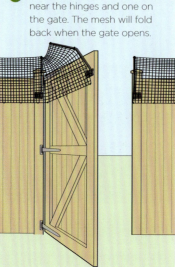

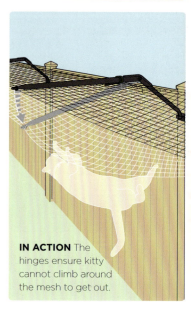

IN ACTION The hinges ensure kitty cannot climb around the mesh to get out.

122 LET KITTY GROOM

Your cat is a professional beautician, spending a great number of her waking hours taking care of herself. She uses her rough tongue to keep her coat clean and silky. When your kitty grooms, she's also regulating her body temperature, getting rid of loose fur while stimulating new fur growth, and occasionally fending off pests like fleas, ticks, and other parasites. Cats seem to take pleasure in grooming themselves, just as we like a nice hot bath or a trip to the spa. If you notice she grooms less than usual (look out for icky odors or matted hair), or does it too much (creating bald spots from overzealous licks), something may be wrong: ask your vet.

123 CONTROL THOSE TUMBLEWEEDS!

Oh, the dreaded hairball. With your cat's ever-so-thorough cleansing habits comes the risk of her swallowing her own hair, and then vomiting it up later as you look on in horror. Long-haired cats are especially prone to developing hairballs. Over-the-counter hairball remedies are available in pet stores—though some vets frown on them—and some cat food is marketed as formulated to keep hairballs at bay. Your first resort, though, should be to buy a cat brush and help your cat keep her coat free of loose hair, mats, and clumps.

124 KEEP YOUR HOME SMELLING GOOD

Cats have a natural instinct to be clean. This includes grooming themselves with their tongues and carefully burying their bowel movements. Keeping your home clean will reinforce these handy instincts while, of course, benefiting you as well. No one wants a stinky house.

CLEAN BOXES Make sure to clean your cat's litter box daily and replace the litter entirely every few weeks (*see* item 022).

VACUUM CARPETS Make sure you vacuum cat fur from the floor and furniture regularly. This will prevent smells and dirt from building up.

WIPE SURFACES Regularly wash and wipe surfaces, such as hardwood or laminate flooring, doors, and baseboards to keep them clean and reduce odors,

WASH BOWLS Food remains can be very smelly. It is crucial to the health and well-being of your cat that you clean food bowls after every meal.

LAUNDER FABRICS All home fabrics, including curtains, bedspreads, and tablecloths, can hold on to odors, so be sure to wash them frequently.

STORE SUPPLIES Designating a cupboard, room—or even a sliver of apartment space—for your cat's supplies, such as food and litter, will reduce clutter and prevent their odor from spreading.

125 HANDLE THE HOLIDAYS

While you might enjoy them, holidays can be terrifying for cats. Both indoor and outdoor cats can become upset at unexpected noises, such as fireworks, or scared of a houseful of guests. Sometimes they get so flummoxed they flee from home, bolt over fences in a panic, and then find themselves alone and lost. Here are some ideas to keep your kitty happy.

PROVIDE SANCTUARY Before any holidays or celebrations, bring outdoor cats inside. If they can't be inside, at least make sure they have unobstructed access to a secure, enclosed place where they can escape any noises. If you're expecting guests, it's best to keep indoor kitties in their own room where they will remain undisturbed. If they're social cats and they're allowed to mingle, make sure your guests don't leave a door open long enough for a cat to dart outside and get lost!

LET CATS BE CATS Although it's become popular to dress up pets for certain holidays (especially Halloween), it's better to leave the costumes to the humans. If you absolutely must dress up your pet, make sure the costume isn't made from toxic materials, and keep your cat safely confined. You may think he looks hilarious, however, he may be very stressed and unhappy to be restrained in some silly costume.

KEEP THEM SAFE Numerous human holiday foods, such as chocolate, raisins, and rich foods, are toxic to cats and dogs (*see* item 016). Candies may be a choking hazard, while the foil tinsel used to decorate Christmas trees can pose a serious risk to cats if ingested. Holiday plants like poinsettias are extremely poisonous (*see* item 018). Be sure such foods and "toys" are out of your cat's reach during the holidays.

126
TEST YOUR KITTY IQ

Cats are endlessly fascinating creatures and it pays off to learn all you can about them and their habits. When you've been sharing your home with a cat for a while, you might start to think you're a bit of a feline expert. Put your cat knowledge to the test by doing this fun quiz. If you get all six questions correct, then you are well on the way to understanding your purrfect purry companion. If you get fewer than two correct, don't give up, just try the next quiz (see item 163).

1 WHO HAS MORE BONES?

☐ Humans

☐ Cats

☐ Horses

2 WHOSE HEARING IS KEENEST?

☐ Humans

☐ Cats

☐ Horses

3 WHAT IS THE TECHNICAL NAME FOR A CAT LOVER?

☐ Ailurophile

☐ Kittehlovah

☐ Tabbyfanitis

4 WHAT MAMMAL HAS THE LARGEST EYES, RELATIVE TO SIZE?

☐ Cats

☐ Humans

☐ Mice

5 CATS SEE BETTER IN THE DARK THAN HUMANS DO. HOW MUCH BETTER?

☐ Four times better

☐ Six times better

☐ Eleven times better

6 BESIDES COMMUNICATION, WHAT IS ANOTHER USE OF A CAT'S TAIL?

☐ It helps with balance

☐ It can flick away flies

☐ It acts as a weapon against other animals

ANSWERS

1 Cats! While humans have 206 bones, cats have 230. **2** The answer is cats. They're such superheroes, aren't they? **3** The answer is ailurophile, from the Greek "ailuros," (cat), and philos, (beloved, loving). **4** You thought it was you, didn't you? Nope. It's kitty! **5** Cats see six times better in the dark than we do. **6** The answer is balance. How cool is that?

127

DISTINGUISH BODY TYPES

Whereas dogs vary greatly in size from a Great Dane to a Chihuahua, cats are more or less all the same size. Or are they? It's true that the variation between different cat types and breeds is not as marked as it is in dogs, but there are large cats and small cats—and there are cats with long legs and others with very short legs.

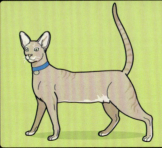

SHORT AND COBBY
The Munchkin is one of several breeds with very short legs. They make do with climbing and clambering rather than jumping.

TALL AND SLIM
The legs of Orientals and Siamese seem to be long but this is probably due to their slight bodies and their elegant movement.

LARGE AND FLUFFY
Norwegian Forest Cats and Maine Coons are very big cats. Their thick coats also contribute to their impressive presence.

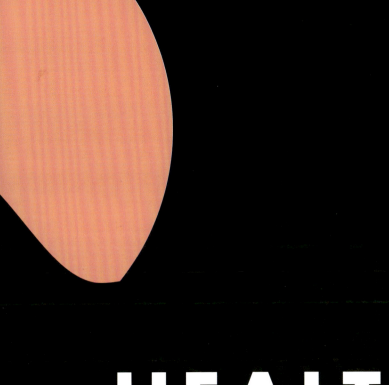

HEALTH

> "A cat has absolute emotional honesty: human beings, for one reason or another, may hide their feelings, but a cat does not."
>
> **ERNEST HEMINGWAY**

A cat can live as many as twenty years—or even more—but to have a long and healthy life, she needs your help. The most important thing you can do to prolong her life is to keep her indoors with plenty of fun and stimulation in her daily activities. She also needs regular vet checkups to ensure she is healthy and up to date on vaccines. You will need to keep her teeth clean, and make sure she is free of fleas and other parasites. A healthy cat should eat well, but should be lean and not overweight. Cats sleep much of the time, but should never be lethargic. Expect your cat to be active, curious, and responsive when she is awake.

Watch out for changes. Your cat needs you to notice unusual behavior that might indicate she is ill, because the sooner you spot a problem and deal with it, the less of a problem it will be. Remember, your cat can't easily tell you when she is not feeling well—cats have evolved to not show pain or distress until it has become acute, so you need to observe her and get to know her in a healthy state. That way, you will be able to easily spot any subtle changes that might suggest something is wrong—and take action early to get her feeling like herself again.

128 VET YOUR VET

Choosing a veterinarian for your cat is a lot like choosing a pediatrician for your child. Like babies, our much-loved animals can let us know they're unhappy, but they can't tell us what is wrong with them or where it hurts, so we rely on vets to do their best detective work, hunting down problems big and small.

GET THE RIGHT PLACE When choosing a vet, it's important to consider the basics, such as proximity to your home, cost for an office visit, and reputation. Getting a recommendation from a cat owner you trust is the absolute best way to find a vet. Find out whether the office or clinic has onsite testing facilities such as X-ray and ultrasound machines. A competent veterinary office should be able to cater to most feline health issues that may arise. Ask about the vet's views on holistic versus traditional medicine, vaccines, and nutrition, and see if they align with your own beliefs.

PICK THE RIGHT PERSON It's very important that you feel comfortable with your cat's doctor. You'll want to find someone who takes the time to answer your questions, someone who makes you feel like he truly cares about your beloved kitty. If your vet always seems preoccupied and eager to move on to the next patient, consider getting a new vet, one who focuses solely on your kitty when she's on the exam table.

TREAT YOUR VET RIGHT Know that the relationship goes both ways. Keep your appointments, pay on time, and schedule routine appointments to keep your cat healthy, and your vet will love you!

129 PREPARE FOR VET TRIPS

If you dread taking your cat to the vet, you're not alone. Many cats freak out on at the prospect of a veterinary visit. With a little work, however, you can help to minimize your cat's concerns.

BE HANDS-ON A cat who is used to being handled will be a chilled-out dude on the vet's table. Routine handling at home benefits his health, too—by giving your cat a regular at-home head-to-toe examination, you will spot issues that need attention.

PLAY BEFORE LEAVING An hour or two before departing for the vet, calm your kitty down by petting and playing with her. Keep it light-hearted and casual.

SCHEDULE STRATEGICALLY Try to schedule an appointment on a weekday, but not at lunchtime. That way, you can avoid the risk of a crowded waiting room, which could unnerve your cat before her examination.

130

MINIMIZE CARRIER TERROR

Yikes! How can so much howling and hissing come from one little cat? Fiercely protective of their freedom, cats usually resist being cooped up, to the point where your kitty might sound like you're torturing him when he catches the mere sight of his carrying basket. To reduce his fear, try keeping the carrier out in the open at home, so he can sniff it, paw at it, and maybe even lounge in it casually. The trick is to link it to everyday life, not those traumatic trips to the vet's office where he'll be poked and prodded. Offering him treats inside the carrier is the icing on the cake.

Use a carrier large enough for your kitty to stand up and turn around inside. Add his favorite cushion or an item of your clothing. With a little time and patience, he just might make peace with his once-dreaded carrier.

FACT OR FICTION?

CATS ARE LONERS
Despite the fact that cats enjoy alone time (not to mention naptime), they are very social. It's been proven time and again that cats are happiest with pals. Those pals may be other kitties, dogs, humans, or all of the above. But they are definitely social animals. Maybe that's why they're so popular on social media!

131 SPICE IT UP

Cats can be picky eaters. But did you know that you can train your cat to be less finicky simply by varying her diet? It's true! A well-rounded diet that relies on multiple sources of protein can also prevent allergies and is good for your cat's general well-being. Offering her some variety can be a simple matter of combining wet food with dry food or picking several flavors of cans or sachets from the pet-store shelves. Shop around, and try to find five different flavors or types of food (or even more!) that appeal to your kitty. Then keep them in the regular rotation in your kitchen. Yum!

132
KNOW WHAT KITTY NEEDS

Cats are carnivores, which means that protein is a key source of energy. Purina scientists have conducted nutrition studies to show that cats readily use carbohydrates for energy as well, and most major cat food brands also contain some vegetables to create a complete and balanced diet. A cat food containing high protein will feed a domesticated cat's natural instincts.

133
MAKE IT BALANCE

What does your cat need to eat to remain strong and healthy? Here's a rundown:

• Proteins come from animal and plant sources. Cats need certain amino acids that are found only in animal products. Proteins offer amino acids that build and heal body tissues and cells.
• Fats keep your cat's coat silky and aid in fat-soluble vitamin absorption.
• Carbohydrates supply energy, while preserving amino acids for important functions like immune health.
• Vitamins and minerals support the immune system, keep your cat's coat shiny and healthy, and play an important role in many other body functions.
• And water (*see* item 137)

The route to a well-nourished kitty-cat? Become a voracious label reader and ensure your cat's diet provides complete and balanced nutrition; when in doubt, ask your vet for advice.

134 COUNT THE CALORIES

As with all animals, cats need higher-calorie foods as babies, and fewer calories during middle age. While the nutrient requirements for healthy seniors are similar to those of younger adult cats, some older cats benefit from a more energy-dense kibble to receive adequate nutrition. High protein is also good to maintain lean body mass in seniors. Many older cats have an inability to properly digest and utilize dietary fats, so a reduced fat diet is not recommended.

135 BE WARY OF HOME COOKING

Be very careful when attempting to make your own cat foods. You may have the best of intentions, but a homemade diet may not be the best option for your cat.

We recommend sticking to commercial, ready-made cat food, since most contain the right balance of the vitamins, minerals, proteins, carbs, and fats your kitty needs to thrive. If you decide to cook for kitty, you may find it hard to achieve that balance. If the homemade alternative is of real interest to you, talk to your vet to ensure it's best for your kitty. Please note that many foods in our pantries can harm our cats, and it's vital they don't eat them (*see* item 016 for more information).

136 KEEP PAWS CLEAN

Danger alert! If you use clay clumping litter in your litter box, your cat may get it stuck on his paws, which may lead to him licking them clean and ingesting the litter. In large enough doses, this habit may cause intestinal obstruction. If you see your cat dutifully grooming himself and getting a mouthful of litter in the process, swoop in and clean his paws while firmly saying "No." To be extra careful, especially if your cat seems bent on paw cleaning, consider replacing clumping litter with recycled newspaper or special pellets.

137 KEEP KITTY WELL WATERED

On average, a ten-pound (5-kg) cat needs about a cup of fresh water daily, and more in hot weather. Be sure to supply a clean bowl containing at least this much fresh water per-cat per-day, in addition to food.

GIVE DIFFERENT FLUIDS If your cat doesn't drink much, don't panic. If she has wet food, some of her liquid intake will come from this. If she only eats dry food (which obviously has a low water content), try to get her to eat canned food as well. If she's fussy, try different flavors, and warm the food to enhance its appeal.

KEEP IT CLEAN Make the water as appealing as possible. Due to her amazing sense of smell, even day-old water may arouse your kitty's disdain, so rinse and refill her water dish daily and thoroughly wash it at least twice a week. Consider keeping the water dish some distance from the food dish to keep stray crumbs from getting in it (oh, the horror!). Note that plastic retains odors and bacteria, so your picky kitty may prefer her water in porcelain, glass, or stainless steel bowls.

OFFER CHOICE Do you give your cat spring water blessed by monks, but she prefers to drink from a dripping faucet? This is because the faucet mimics the motion of water in nature (which, she instinctively knows, keeps it fresh). It's fine for your cat to drink it, as long as your tap water meets health standards. Another option is to purchase a cat water-fountain, where continually filters and recycles the water. Keep the fountain clean, and replace the water as recommended by the manufacturer.

AVOID MILK While many a cat has been depicted lapping up a bowl of milk in quaint folk art paintings and cartoons, in fact, cats can't digest cow's milk very well (*see* also item 070) so don't give it, even as a treat.

138 EARN YOUR STRIPES

Cats come in all sorts of colors. And cat hairs can have three or more colors along a single shaft. It is interesting how colors affect a cat's appearance. Spots and stripes, for example, are good for camouflage, while "points" or "shades," terms often used in describing pedigree cat colors, make their owner stand out in a crowd!

TABBY
A cat is never "just a tabby". His stripes are usually darker than the rest of his fur and can be mackerel, swirled, spotted, or ticked.

POINTED
Pointed cats are those with pale body fur and darker legs, tails, and faces. The hair contains an enzyme which makes cooler fur darker!

SMOKEY, SHADED, AND TICKED
This refers to hair that has different colours along its length, so it might be dark at the root, paler in the middle, and dark again at the tip.

139 SPOT THE SYMPTOMS

Because your cat is a private creature, it may be hard to tell when she's feeling under the weather. Cats like to keep their problems to themselves and won't usually walk up to you, whine, and ask for help. And so identifying an ailing kitty means looking carefully for signs and signals, or any hint that she's acting differently. Trust your instincts. If you think she's off color, she probably is. When observing your cat's behavior, ask yourself whether she is:

SIGNS OF SICKNESS

- Hiding more often than usual and/or in different places
- Acting more energetic, or less active, than usual
- Eating more or less than usual Not touching her favorite food
- Drinking much more water than usual or hardly drinking anything at all
- Suffering from bad breath (or worse-than-usual breath)
- Waking up in the night or disturbing you at odd times
- Taking catnaps during the day (if she's usually energetic)
- Clinging to you (She might be uncomfortable)
- Ignoring you, when she's usually a friendly, cuddly cat

Cats are quirky so these signs don't always mean your kitty is ill, but they're worth monitoring. If after a day or two the behavior doesn't return to normal, or even worsens, and there's no obvious external cause (such as houseguests that stress out your creature of habit), consider taking your cat to the vet for a checkup.

140

KNOW COMMON AILMENTS

Cats are prone to several illnesses and conditions, but here's the good news: with just a little attention from your veterinarian (plus your TLC) a cat can usually come back swingin'.

Cats, especially those that are stressed or in crowded conditions, can get the highly-contagious feline upper respiratory illness (URI), which has cold-like symptoms, such as watery eyes and sneezing (*see* also item 146). Thankfully this is pretty easy for your vet to cure. Fleas are another Achilles' heel for cats—and again, need prompt attention as soon as you spot the symptoms, which include scratching.

Urinary tract diseases (me-oww!!) tend to trouble cats. If you have experienced a urinary tract infection yourself, you know the misery they cause—so please, please get your cat to a vet at the first sign he's straining to urinate, tries to go often and with little result, seems distressed upon urination, or has blood in his urine.

Other common ailments include gastrointestinal problems, such as diarrhea and vomiting, and eye issues like cataracts and glaucoma.

141

KEEP TABS ON THE KIDNEYS

Kidney disease can be common in cats, especially as they get older. In fact, our furry little friends can suffer from not one but two types of kidney disease. And they're both bad. But, if you get to know the symptoms and potential causes of kidney disease, you'll be able to act quickly and effectively if your cat is affected.

Chronic kidney disease usually afflicts cats aged seven and up. It develops slowly, so is difficult to spot, and over time it diminishes kidney function. Treatment usually involves fluid therapy and putting kitty on a special diet (*see* item 155).

Acute kidney disease, in contrast, can strike within weeks or even days. Causes include poisoning, kidney infection or blockage, or heart problems such as low blood pressure or heart failure. Loss of blood or a broken pelvis can also cause acute kidney problems. While acute kidney disease sounds scary, it can usually be cured with prompt treatment.

142 ADDRESS SERIOUS ILLNESS CALMLY

Hearing your vet say, "I'm sorry, but your cat is very ill" may seem like your worst nightmare. There's no sugar-coating it: if your cat has a serious illness, such as renal failure, feline distemper, or leukemia, the road ahead may be hard and long, not to mention potentially expensive and fraught with difficult decisions. If you get bad news about your cat's health, first take a deep breath and give your cat a cuddle, then start to explore your treatment options as calmly and as fully as possible. Listen carefully to what your vet tells you. Staying clear-headed will help you choose the best treatment for your kitty. Remember to take care of yourself, too. Talk to friends and family and take it one day at a time. You can get through this. You are stronger than you think.

143 CARE FOR ARTHRITIS

Like people, cats can suffer from arthritis, a condition where joints swell, flexibility decreases, and the body feels stiff. Usually, arthritis strikes with age, but infections or trauma to the body can also cause it.

Beyond prescription medication, you can help your arthritic kitty feel better by making her life, well, cushier. A cat with arthritis will find it uncomfortable to run up and down stairs and leap after prey the way she used to do. Ensure that she can get to her food, water, and litter box without having to perform acrobatic feats (ouch).

Surround her with soft blankets and pad her bed with pillows. Help her groom parts of her body that she's straining to reach—and give her lots and lots of TLC. For example, regular massages may help soothe your pretty kitty. Other outlets to explore are acupuncture and water therapy; while these may seem somewhat unconventional (and counter to cats' natural aversion to water and, let's face it, needles), many cat guardians have reported great improvement in their kitties' symptoms and an increase in activity after trying such remedies.

144 HEAD OFF HERPES

Yes, we said herpes! Cats get it, too. Two viruses cause feline herpes: feline viral rhinopneumonitis (FVR) and feline herpesvirus type 1 (FHV-1). They affect your cat's eyes or upper respiratory system. Pink, irritated eyes, inflamed eyelids, and eye ulcers and lesions can be symptoms, as can sneezing and drooling, in addition to the standard something's-wrong-with-kitty fare of appetite changes, clinginess, and depression. Being in close contact with infected cats (mutual grooming, sharing a litter box, or living in crowded quarters

with other cats) puts your kitty at risk for this highly-contagious virus. Don't be worried about your health: humans and other animals cannot catch feline herpes.

Most cats who catch feline herpes will not show symptoms except for when they first get it and during occasional outbreaks. They will, however, carry the virus for life, but the symptoms can be managed with simple medications, when and if they occur. And the best news? Staying up-to-date on vaccinations can prevent your kitty from contracting FVR or FHV-1 in the first place!

145 STOP STOMATITIS ASAP

Stomatitis is a big word to describe inflammation of your kitty's little mouth. It's pretty common, painful as heck, and potentially dangerous to your kitty's long-term health, so look out for any warning signs and do your cat a favor—get him to the vet as soon as possible if you see symptoms including:

- Pink, inflamed, or even bleeding gums;
- Bad breath (caused by inflamed tissues);
- Difficulty swallowing food and water.

Your cat may need long-term treatment to keep the symptoms at bay. Act quickly and you may prevent the inflammation from spreading or getting worse. Treatments include antibiotics, supplements, and tooth extraction.

146 TREAT RESPIRATORY DISEASES

Bacteria and viruses can cause nasty upper respiratory infection (URI) in our cats—boo! Runny noses and eyes, nasal discharge, changes in appetite, and fever all scream, "Get thee to the vet!"

Respiratory viruses are contagious from cat to cat and have an incubation period of two to seven days, but troublingly, even cats who have recovered from infections can remain carriers, and may transmit infection to other kitties, long afterward.

Treatment involves antibiotics (and fluid therapy in some cases), plus plenty of TLC. This is where you can help your cat's recovery. Encourage her to eat, keep her warm, and wipe away any discharge from eyes and nose. Soon she'll be on the road to health.

147 FIGHT URINARY TRACT ATTACKS!

Urinary tract issues are very common in cats. Your cat won't obviously complain about the discomfort in his bladder, so be sure to watch for any warning signs. Is he urinating much more than usual, and continuing to try to pee while there is little to no urine come out? Maybe he's licking around his urinary area, as if trying to ease pain? Is he eating less, or acting sluggish, nervous, or ultra-clingy? When he urinates, do you see blood? Act immediately. If you suspect a urinary tract attack, don't wait to see if it gets worse. Be safe rather than sorry, and spirit your cat away to the vet for some relief. He will thank you! If your kitty experiences chronic urinary tract infections, there are supplements and special diets that can help to prevent flare-ups.

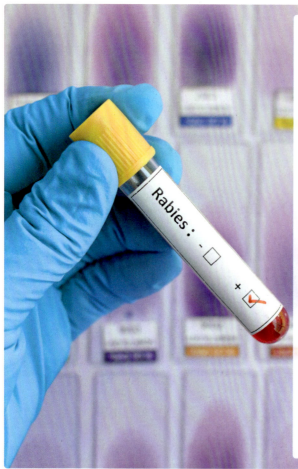

148

BE SMART ABOUT INFECTIOUS DISEASES

Thinking about all the infectious diseases out there—diseases that could cause your kitty pain and suffering—is enough to boggle the mind of any loving cat parent. From rabies to distemper to FIV (*see* item 149), there are oh so many threats to your dear kitty's health! But don't fret: knowledge is power when it comes to prevention and management of nasty illnesses.

To a large extent, indoor cats are shielded from the infectious diseases they could catch from other kitties, whether domestic or stray. They're also pretty much protected from fleas, ticks, and other parasitic infections, and they tend to live longer than outdoor cats! So if you're a squeamish or very protective cat parent, keeping your kitty indoors should make you (both) feel better. Indoor cats are not magically immune to disease, though, and should still be taken to the vet for checkups.

Above all, the best thing you can do for your cat's health is learn about the illnesses described in this chapter and hope they don't strike, but be ready to pounce into action if they do.

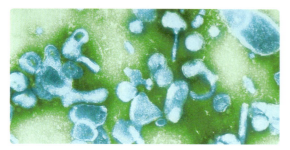

149

STAND AGAINST FIV AND FELV

Like HIV in humans, feline immunodeficiency virus (FIV) and feline leukemia virus (FeLV) compromise a cat's immune systems and make him susceptible to a variety of problematic secondary infections.

FIV is transmitted cat-to-cat, usually through bite wounds inflicted during a fight (a perfect reason to keep your cat safely indoors), although sometimes an FIV-positive mother cat can transmit the virus to her kittens during their birth. Although there is no treatment for the virus itself, it leaves your cats susceptible to secondary infections, which can be treated, and the disease can be managed with regular vet care and a proper diet.

FeLV is highly transmissible through bodily fluids like blood, urine, and saliva, and can be passed from cat to cat through sharing of water bowls and litter boxes, and through mutual grooming.

Vaccinations for both FIV and FeLV are available, so ask your veterinarian about these as soon as you adopt your kitty. It's also important to note that neither virus can be passed to humans or non-feline animals. Finally, if your cat is diagnosed with either FIV or FeLV, take heart—he can still live a long, healthy life with the right care.

150 GET THROUGH CHEMO

Cats who fight cancer are little heroes. While chemotherapy is no fun for your kitty, you may find that she's surprisingly tolerant of it while it does what it's supposed to do. Chemo can be very unpleasant for people, but for cats, the side effects are comparatively mild. In fact, many cat owners report that the hardest part of chemotherapy for their cats seems to be the car ride to the vet's office! However, a decrease in appetite, as well as vomiting and diarrhea are typical in kitties that are undergoing chemo. As the medicine fights your cat's cancer cells, make sure you manage any unpleasant side effects, keep her appetite up by feeding her food she loves, and just plain spoil her rotten!

151 KEEP UP WITH VACCINES

The core feline vaccines for cats are those that protect against feline herpesvirus 1 (FHV-1), feline calicivirus (FCV), feline panleukopenia virus (FPV), and rabies. Ask your vet which of these are appropriate for your cat, and that may depend on whether he is allowed outdoors and will be exposed to other animals. Like human babies, to begin with, kittens need multiple sets of booster shots so that they get full protection. It's important, too, to keep up with vaccines in adult cats, who typically also need boosters every three years.

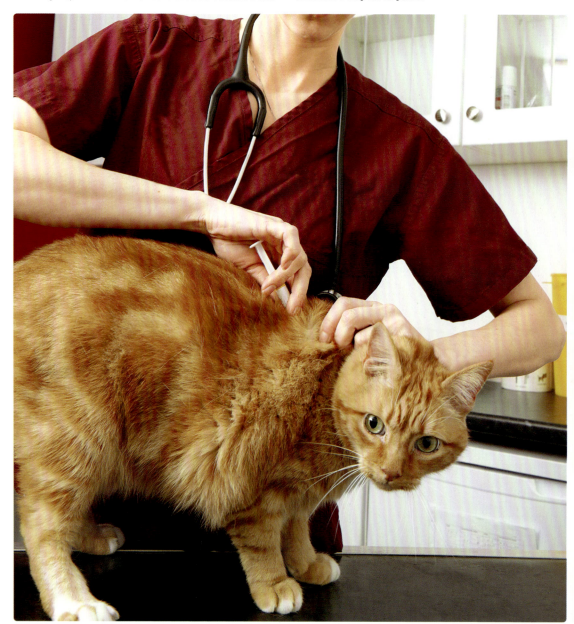

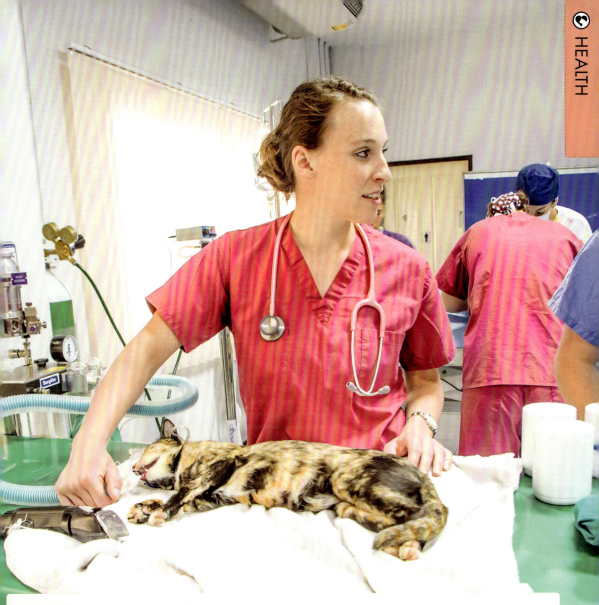

152 CONSIDER HOSPITAL CARE

What does a pet parent do when a cat gets really sick, so sick that he needs to be kept away from anything that could affect his delicate immune system? In such cases, you may need to choose between looking after your cat at home or having him stay at a pet hospital. The first option probably seems tempting: you'll get to see and look after pet your sick kitty every day and night. And you'll save hundreds or sometimes thousands in hospital bills (unless you have some awesome pet insurance). But, despite the expense, a hospital stay has some real pluses. In a hospital, your cat is guaranteed to get constant monitoring and fast professional action if anything should go wrong.

So think twice—maybe three times—about that hospital stay, as it may be the best thing for your much-loved pet's health.

153 MANAGE CARE COSTS

When a cat has a serious illness or injury, the costs of medical care can get very high very quickly. There's examination and lab tests, then X-rays and MRIs, to say nothing of medications and hospital stays . . . the tab adds up. You want what's best for your dear kitty, but you're only human, and you may not have the resources to spare. Here are some straightforward tips for softening the blow while still getting the best care for your cat:

NEGOTIATE A PAYMENT PLAN Many veterinarians will be open to an arrangement where you spread your payments out over months or even years, if you can't, or would rather not, take a big financial hit all at once.

LOOK INTO ASSISTANCE There are some non profit organizations whose sole function is to provide emergency veterinary funding. Google "emergency veterinary funding" to find any resources available to help you.

START A CROWDFUNDING PAGE More and more, people set up crowdfunding pages to allow friends and family to donate to cat-care expenses in exchange for photos of the patient and regular updates. Don't be afraid to ask! Post a link to your crowdfunding page on your social media channels; you may be pleasantly surprised by how many people are willing to kick in a few dollars.

MAKE MONEY CREATIVELY Can you sell some old clothes you were going to throw away, maybe in a yard sale? Can you do some overtime at work? If you earn money from a source you weren't counting on before, it'll feel like a bonus, which you can put toward the best cause imaginable.

154 INVESTIGATE INSURANCE

It is a very good idea to sign your cat up for pet health insurance before you have a medical expense that may not be covered because it is a "pre-existing condition". There are many pet health insurance companies, offering different types of plans. Some are dirt cheap, and—be warned—cover next to nothing, while pricier ones promise to protect your wallet from all the big vet expenses. Consider how much you can afford on insurance premiums and the amount you might have to pay from your own pocket in a worst-case senario. If you work for a large company, you might get a discount. Look at insurance programs very carefully. While few will cover every single eventuality, insurance is worth considering (and shopping around for). Even if you don't use it to the max, it'll give you peace of mind. Ask your vet which plans they find offer the best coverage.

155 REVIEW YOUR MEDICATION OPTIONS

Suppose your cat has just had surgery or dental work, or needs medication for any other reason. It helps to know a bit about it. Cat medication comes in various forms:

- Injections, IVs, and subcutaneous fluids
- Pills
- Liquids
- Gels
- Specially formulated food

Most injections are one-off and will be done at the vet's office. However, with some illnesses, such as kidney disease, intravenous (IV) fluid therapy is given at your vet's office, and then needs to be followed by ongoing subcutaneous (sometimes called "sub-Q") fluid treatments. Some pet parents learn how to give shots or administer sub-Q fluids so they can treat their kitty at home. Not everyone is up for this, so don't feel bad if you're not! Discuss your options with your vet to determine what's best.

Other medication can be given at home with some simple techniques. Here are a few guidelines:

PILLS You may be able to crush these and add them to your cat's wet food. Or, hide them in a "pill pocket" cat treat. Otherwise, you'll need to get kitty to "pop" them. Try using a pet piller, a special tool that shoots the pill to the back of your cat's throat, increasing the chance that he'll swallow it. (Item 157 has more on pill-giving).

LIQUID Some medicine can be administered in liquid form. It helps if it is pleasantly flavored since this makes it easier to persuade kitty to take it. While you might be tempted to put it on her food, this could just mean wasted food and wasted medicine. Item 156 discusses how to give liquid medication calmly and safely.

GEL Some medication (such as Methimazole, which is used to treat thyroid disease) is available as a transdermal gel that's rubbed inside the cat's ear. If your little patient needs this type of medicine, the vet will show you how to apply it. Other gels include those for hairballs, which you can administer like liquid medicines.

FOOD Typically your cat will have to eat a prescription food for the rest of her life, although some such foods are intended as pick-me-ups after illness. Your vet will probably have them, or can tell you where to purchase them. Cats don't always like these diets, and you may have to try different types to find one your cat will eat.

156 ADMINISTER LIQUID MEDICINE WITH EASE

So you think the hard part is over: you and your cat finally get home after a vet visit with a bottle of liquid medication and an accompanying syringe or dropper. (If you have a syringe, this will allow you to push the medicine into your cat's mouth more quickly, while a dropper will administer the medicine a little more slowly.) Surprise! The hard part lies ahead. Here's how to make giving medicine a little bit easier.

STEP 1 Fill the dropper or syringe with the prescribed amount (A). Always double-check that the amount you are about to give is the correct dose.

STEP 2 Restrain your cat, either by holding him firmly but comfortably, or by wrapping him in a towel or throw with just his head showing (B)—like a kitty burrito! Hold him gently against you. Talk to your cat cheerfully and soothingly the whole time. As we've mentioned already (see item 082), cats learn to recognize phrases, such as, "It's OK," "Good kitty," and so on, and this is a good time to put that recognition to use.

STEP 3 Hold his head still with one hand, and insert the tip of the dropper or syringe into a corner of his mouth (C) between his cheek and teeth. Be careful not to tilt his head back, since he could inhale the medicine. This is of particular concern with kittens or weak cats.

STEP 4 Aim the dropper or syringe toward the back of his head and gently squeeze or push the plunger until the full dose of liquid medication is in his mouth.

STEP 5 Stroke his neck a few times, starting just below the chin, so that he swallows. Do this before you let him go, otherwise he'll skip off and spit everything out—probably on your new sofa—before you can stop him.

STEP 6 Remember to reward your patient cat with one of his favorite treats! (D)

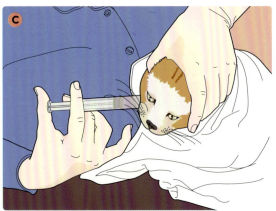

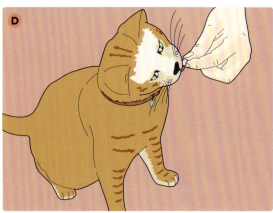

157 GIVE A CAT A PILL (AND LIVE!)

You may think that giving your cat a pill requires a hazmat suit and a whole lot of alcohol (for you!). But it doesn't have to be traumatic. Here are some suggestions about how to make it a simple, quick, and comfortable task.

1 Before you get started, prepare a "chaser" of wet food, broth, or water and have it on hand to give immediately after your kitty takes her pill. Or try baby food, as long as it's free of onion and garlic, which are toxic to cats.

2 Coat the pill with butter or a cat-approved oil like sunflower oil or high-quality fish oil. This lubrication will make swallowing much easier.

3 As with giving liquid medicine (opposite), wrap your cat in a towel so that just her head is showing, and hold her against you.

4 If the pill is flavored, try presenting it to your cat as a treat. She might take it. If not open her mouth with one hand, then quickly insert the pill with the other.

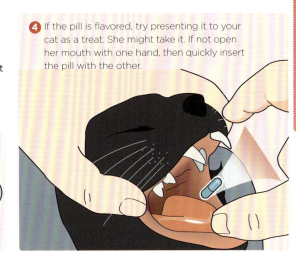

5 Hold her mouth closed until she swallows the pill, stroking her neck a few times to help it go down. Follow up with the appetizing chaser just to sweeten the deal.

6 Beware: a dry pill can get lodged in a cat's throat, leading to serious complications, so if she doesn't want to take a food or water chaser, gently syringe a teaspoon of water into one corner of her mouth.

158 EXPLORE HOLISTIC MEDICINE

Let's say your cat is suffering from a chronic ailment such as arthritis or FIV: you're following a treatment plan with your vet, but your kitty still seems out of sorts. Or say your cat's been depressed, lethargic, or jumpy, and your vet has run every test under the sun and pronounced him healthy, yet he doesn't seem that way. Here's another scenario: your lucky kitty is fit as a fiddle, and you want to make sure he stays that way. Holistic treatments such as herbal medicines, homeopathic remedies, acupuncture, and massage therapies are all options for expanding your cat's repertoire of health tools. Just be sure to check with your vet first, and ask the holistic practitioner about potential side effects and drug interactions—and remember that many holistic practices are not strictly regulated like veterinary medicine, so to protect your kitty, proceed with caution and common sense.

159 MAKE FLEAS FLEE!

There are many ways to keep fleas and other pests at bay. Among the most effective pest repellents are topical liquids that you apply monthly between your kitty's shoulder blades. Ask your vet to recommend the best products to use, and never exceed the recommended dosage.

Other ways to make fleas flee: super-clean your home from top to bottom, give your cat a bath in baby shampoo; and comb your kitty's fur with a special flea comb. Unfortunately, a bout of fleas usually means tapeworms are on deck, too, so take your cat to the vet to get tested in the next week or two, or ask your vet to recommend a dewormer.

160 LICK THOSE TICKS!

Ticks are nasty little critters. Once they latch on to your cat's skin, they suck blood out—and if not removed, they can cause serious illness. Certain medications can be applied to your cat's coat, protecting her from ticks for up to a month. (It's a good idea to ask your vet to recommend one.) Otherwise, when it comes to licking ticks, you can score yet another point by giving your kitty a regular massage—using this time to also check her thoroughly for ticks. Remove any ticks you find using fine-tipped tweezers or a special tick-removal tool. To avoid leaving the tick's head embedded in her skin, which can cause infection, ask your veterinarian to show you how to remove them efficiently using either technique.

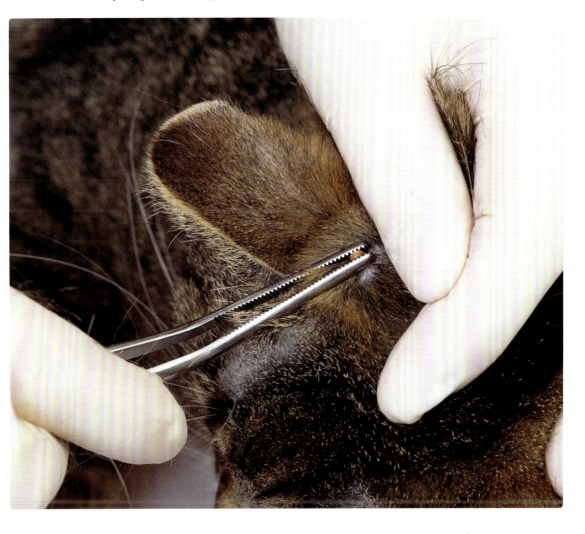

DOUBLE-O CAT

There is hardly a person alive who doesn't know that the villain of the 007 movies, Ernst Stavro Blofeld, always appears with a fluffy white cat. The cat in question has been played by several different cats due to the number of years the James Bond franchise has been going. He has no name—although he is rumored to be called Tiddles.

BIRTH NAME
Maybe Tiddles, but who knows?

FILMS
Many James Bond movies.

BOOKS
The World According to Blofeld's Cat

OTHER MEDIA
Many clips on YouTube; he also has a Twitter account under the pseudonym Blofeld's Cat.

TRIVIA
Several movie bad-guys have been inspired by Double-O Cat, including Han in Bruce Lee's *Enter the Dragon* and Dr Evil in *Austin Powers*. The 2001 animated film *Cats & Dogs* stars a wicked white modern Persian who is called Mr Tinkles. The idea of a cat-loving villain probably comes from Cardinal Richelieu in Andre Dumas's *The Three Musketeers*.

Blofeld's cat is a long-haired, "traditional" Persian (so-called because he has a pointed face, while modern Persians are known for their flat-faced good looks). This fated feline first appeared in *From Russia with Love* in 1963. He was such a star that his presence on screen became symbolic of his master: in *Thunderball* and *For Your Eyes Only*, all that is shown is Blofeld's hand stroking Tiddles; Blofeld doesn't appear. The poor kitty had to witness an exploding operations room in *You Only Live Twice*. A popular You Tube clip reveals his reaction and some brave acting by his co-star. Thankfully, nowadays, a cat would not be expected to go through that sort of trauma. In *Spectre* the white cat decides he rather likes James Bond, which makes bad-tempered Blofeld even crosser than usual!

In the James Bond books by Ian Fleming, Blofeld does not have a cat, but that other wicked character, Goldfinger, has a ginger pussycat—well, he likes all things golden!

161 TAKE CARE OF YOUR ELDERS

As your cat gets older, he'll slow down. He'll likely loose some weight and muscle mass, and will not be able to keep his coat as well groomed as he used to. This is a chance for you to show your love for your friend and give him some special care.

GIVE A MASSAGE This is soothing, but it also helps prevent hairballs (if you use a gentle brush to assist in your massage), increases your cat's circulation, and ensures you're familiar with his body—so you can detect, and act on, any lumps you may find.

KEEP AN EYE Is he eating less, drinking more, sleeping more, or using the litter box more or less often? Older cats may alter their habits, but watch out for extreme changes that may signal a developing disease.

ENCOURAGE EXERCISE Older cats love to lounge around, but they'll appreciate it even more if they're in good health. Help keep your elder active with gentle play sessions.

162 GIVE SPACE AND LOVE

If your cat has been at the vet's office and especially if she has had a procedure or been there for several days, be sure to exactly follow the instructions your vet gives about feeding and medication when she gets home. Don't hesitate to call your vet if you have questions.

Your poor kitty will likely need some quiet time to adjust, so make sure she has a safe place at home where other animals (or kids) can't bother her. She may smell odd and perhaps have bandages on her, too, and this can cause other cats to hiss or be aggressive, so be sure to keep her separate from them if you see any of this type of behavior. Remember, visiting the vet can be very stressful for a cat and she may have gotten little sleep, so give her space and time to recover.

CARE

> "Dogs believe they are human.
> Cats believe they are God."
>
> UNKNOWN

Caring for a cat is relatively easy. Most days, a cat doesn't need much from you aside from the physical basics: fresh water, fresh food, shelter, a clean litter box, and, of course, love. Caring for a cat can be so easy, in fact, that sometimes people neglect to spend that extra time interacting with their furry friend. Be sure that you put aside a few special minutes each day—maybe before you go to bed—to have quality play and cuddle time. What is fun for a cat can be fun for you. Dangling a toy on a string for him to chase or making a cat maze for him to explore keeps him entertained and fit, and amuses you and your family as you watch his clever acrobatic antics. And if you share your cat's cuteness online, who knows—your kitty might be the next famous cat on the internet.

When you share your life with your cat, you can expect visits to the vet, grooming and claw care, traveling, and any number of daily events that may need your attention. Remember to ask for help and advice when you need it. The world is filled with cat lovers who can help you with tips and tricks—like those you are about to read—that will make it easy to have a great life with your feline family member.

163

EXPAND YOUR KNOWLEDGE

There is so much to know about cats. These fascinating animals have long been part of our lives, probably moving in with us when they discovered we are a source of food, shelter, and warmth. In turn we found cats useful for vermin control. However, complete domestication probably took many centuries, and it is interesting that feral cats can fend quite well for themselves, showing how close to the surface a cat's wild side still is. Check out your cat knowledge with the fun quiz below. Item 126 offers more chances to test your knowledge.

1 HOW MANY SPECIES OF CAT, INCLUDING WILD CATS, ARE THERE?

☐ 26

☐ 37

☐ 43

2 WHAT CHANGED IN HUMAN HISTORY TO ENABLE CATS TO BE DOMESTICATED?

☐ We moved into caves.

☐ We became farmers.

☐ We invented the wheel.

3 WHAT IS THE NAME OF JAPAN'S LUCKY CAT?

☐ Maneki-neko

☐ Kurosawa

☐ Naoki Ryuu

4 HOW MANY FERAL CATS ARE THERE WORLDWIDE?

☐ 50 million

☐ 100 million

☐ 10 million

5 WHO IS FASTEST?

☐ Cats

☐ Humans

☐ Dogs

6 HOW LONG IS A CAT'S PREGNANCY?

☐ 63 days

☐ 68 days

☐ 72 days

ANSWERS

1 37. **2** The answer is we became farmers. **3** Maneki-neko means beckoning cat, and the Japanese believe it brings good fortune. **4** 100 million cats have no home to go to. **5** Dogs can run 45 mph (72.4 kph), cats 30 mph (48.2 kph), humans 27.79 mph (44.72 kph). **6** The answer is 63 days.

164 RESOLVE FOOD DILEMMAS

Your local pet store stocks a multitude of cat food options—all with pretty, colorful labels and the promise of great taste and even better nutrition. With so many choices, where to begin?

Start by figuring out where you stand in terms of wet food versus dry food. Earlier (*see* item 137) we talked about how wet food can be hydrating, benefiting your cat's urinary health, especially if she drinks little water. On the other hand, dry food (kept in a sealed bag or container) is easier to work with and doesn't leave you with so many cans to recycle. Some of your fellow cat caregivers will swear by wet food, while others will just buy dry. The only hard-and-fast rule is to find a kind of food—or, better yet, a yummy wet and dry combo—that works for you and your pet. Ask your vet what he or she recommends, and then experiment until you find a combination that your cat loves and that suits you.

165 MAKE SURE KITTY EATS

For many of us, dieting is tough. Not so, it seems, for our cats. Some cats may not go near their food bowls for long stretches of time—and with no clear cause!

Beware: to stay healthy, cats should eat regularly. Keep an eye on your cat's food habits. If he's avoiding eating, take measures to give him his favorite dishes, coaxing him with treats he loves and plenty of praise. Not eating could signal a medical problem, such as fatty liver disease (hepatic lipidosis), which leads to nausea. So if your cat's turning up his nose at food, and misses more than a couple of meals, it's time to get on the phone with your vet.

166 COOL YOUR CAT

Oh, those kitty quirks. While your cat may say "ho hum" to her water bowl, turn on the tap and she'll come running like someone's just burst open a piñata filled with her favorite candy. And who could blame her? Running water is cool, and in the wild, flowing water signals cleanliness (and drinkability). So your cat's attraction to that running faucet can be chalked up to her feline instincts. In step with her preference for cool water, try slipping a couple of ice cubes in kitty's water bowl or get a water fountain (*see* item 137).

167 RECYCLE CARDBOARD

Pet stores sell all sorts of gadgets to keep your kitty entertained. But wait: do you have any old cardboard boxes stashed in the closet? Then hold on to your cash, because you already have the ultimate toy to keep your cat happy for hours on end. Whether he takes a running leap into a too-narrow box and knocks it over (only to try again . . . and again), nestles all the way under packing popcorn and then pops up to say "surprise," or contorts into a teeny tiny space, chances are your old cardboard box is giving your cat the time of his life. Who knew?

168 AMAZE YOUR CAT

Cats love a maze. You can make one with very little effort and provide yourself, and your cat, with hours of amusement. To create a simple maze, you will need a box made of cardboard or another lightweight and easily cut material, some masking tape, and a pair of scissors. Start by opening the lid of the box.

1 Inside the box, put up some cardboard walls.

2 Cut a window or two in the sides. Make them large enough for kitty to get through.

3 Toss a ball or a few toys inside the box maze.

4 Close the lid.

5 Once your makeshift maze captures kitty's attention—a strategic sprinkling of catnip might do the trick—he'll become fascinated by it!

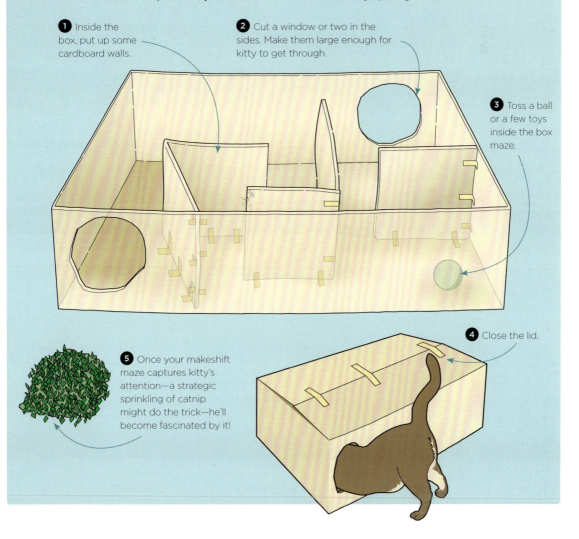

169 PEP UP PLAYTIME

Engaging your cat in healthy, stimulating activities will keep her youthful and healthy, as well as strengthening your bond. Playing also prevents your cat from getting bored, which leads to sluggishness and destructive behavior—decidedly un-fun. Set aside fifteen minutes or so for playtime—you'll have a lot of fun and kitty will thank you. So, no excuses. Here are just a few examples of the many games you can play.

PAPER BAG BOUNCING Put two paper bags on the floor, with their openings facing each other. When your cat enters one bag, scratch the bottom of it and she'll start scuffling like a crazy kitty. Then, scratch the bottom of the other bag and watch her fly out of one bag and into the other. Who knew two paper bags could become an entire playground? She'll enjoy this game time and again.

TRAPPED PREY POUNCING Play on your cat's hunting instincts by tossing a small, light ball into a cardboard box. Your kitty will dive in after it, and then bat it around enthusiastically as if it were prey.

DANCING LIGHT LEAPING Dim the lights and shine a flashlight on walls and furniture. Your cat will dive after the light. To see her chase (or to choreograph a kitty dance routine), simply move the point of light around the room.

170 CRAFT A CAT TENT

A cat tent is yet another fun structure you can make with very little effort and practically no money. You don't need to be a DIY expert, either. It's easy to make something that your cat will love—cats seem to have great imaginations when it comes to pretending to track down prey or hide from scary foes. They can have hours of fun with the simplest of set-ups. Here is one option, but if you want more inspiration, ideas abound on the internet.

1 You need a 15-inch (38-cm) square of cardboard, pliers, masking tape, a T-shirt, two wire hangers, and safety pins

4 Put the ends of the wire through the corner holes. Underneath, fold the wire and put tape over the ends to keep them in place.

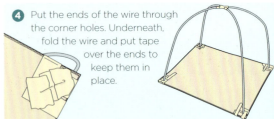

5 Pull the T-shirt over the frame with the head hole at the side.

2 Using the pliers, cut the hooks off both hangers. Bend the hangers into two arches.

6 Turn the tent upside-down. Fold in the arms and fasten them, and other loose parts, with the safety pins.

3 Using the wire, make holes in each corner of the cardboard, about ½ inch (1 cm) from the edge. Tape together the two arches.

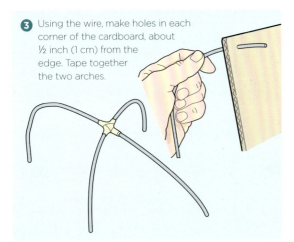

7 Turn the right way up and enjoy watching your cat play inside her new tent.

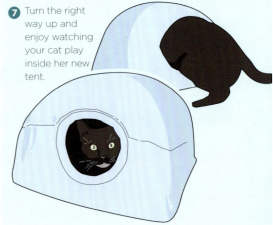

171

PROVIDE A NIP BETWEEN NAPS!

For some kitties, catnip can be oodles of fun. (Watching our cats' crazed reaction is fun for us, too!) The essential oil found in this herb makes some cats act, well . . . weird. If he takes a whiff of it, your cat may freak out. Maybe he'll roll in the stuff, or run around the room. He might even get so worked up that he fiercely protects his prized supply—for about ten minutes, until the catnip's short-lived effect wears off. (But sprinkle some new 'nip on the floor and your cat will react all over again.) Eating catnip, in contrast to sniffing it, makes some cats mellow. Will your cat go crazy for catnip or ignore it completely? That depends on his genetics.

172 TAKE CARE OF TRAVEL BASICS

Whether your cat is flying or traveling by car, train, or bus, she must always be comfortable and secured in a carrier. In every case, make sure she gets adequate water and opportunities to safely use a litter box.

Traveling, and being confined to a carrier, can be stressful for cats. You can attempt to reduce your kitty's stress by spraying a pheromone mist, available at pet supply stores, into her carrier before putting her inside it. You may also consider homeopathic calming herbs formulated for cats, or even a vet-prescribed calming medication. Placing the carrier out in the open, where your cat can see it, a few days prior to travel can also help reduce the amount of stress she suffers when you put her inside it (*see* also items 129 and 130).

173 SET UP SAFE CAR TRIPS

Generally speaking, cats don't make great passengers. And that's an understatement. Sometimes, though, car trips are unavoidable. For those times, here are a few cardinal rules to keep your kitty safe and happy (well, relatively happy).

KEEP KITTY SECURE Always confine your cat safely in a carrier or crate while in the car. It's far too dangerous to allow a kitty to roam loose while your car is in motion; in the event of an accident or a sudden stop, she could be killed or seriously injured. Cats can also suddenly panic during a car trip, distracting or even injuring the driver and causing an accident. And then there's the car window that you forgot to close—this poses a danger whether or not the car is moving.

STAY WITH KITTY Never leave your cat alone in a parked car! Cats are at extreme risk for heat stroke if left in a car for any length of time, even on a day that is warm, rather than hot. Leaving windows open is not enough. Even in shade, a car can quickly warm up and your cat is wearing a fur coat and cannot sweat to cool off. Extreme cold weather can also be dangerous or deadly for cats in cars.

GIVE KITTY WATER Make sure your cat has water throughout the trip. Don't deprive her in order to prevent wetting during your car trip. Many cats can "hold it" for up to twelve hours until they are safely inside a room at their destination. Place a disposable, absorbent urine pad (usually sold in the puppy section of pet supply stores) inside your cat's crate in case of accidents.

174 KIT OUT YOUR CAR

While few cats would include "long-distance road trip" on their bucket list, traveling by car with cats can be more pleasant than you might expect. Careful planning, a little extra pampering, and keeping your cat's routine as regular as possible will go a long way toward keeping you and kitty content on your trip.

If you're traveling with more than one cat, determine ahead of time whether you'll put them together or in separate crates or carriers. Whatever you contain them in, be sure there's room enough for every cat to get up and move around.

PLAY PENS ARE PERFECT If there's enough height in your car, consider a kitty playpen with shelves for perching on, and room on the floor of the pen for a small litter pan. You can buy food and water bowls that attach to the sides of the pen, or attachments for bowls you already own.

CRATES ARE GREAT So long as they are big enough, crates can do the trick. Allot one cat—or a maximum of two—to a crate 25 inches (63 cm) long by 20 inches (50 cm) wide and 20 inches (50 cm) tall, ideally with a shelf or hammock for each cat to sleep in. If there's only room for a small carrier or two, don't panic. Cats often snooze during drives, particularly if they've had kitty-safe calming herbs before departure (*see* item 172).

BREAKS ARE BEST Plan your trip to include regular rest stops, which wll give your cat a break from the endless motion and noise. During breaks, offer her a bowl of water. The stress of a trip can cause cats to pant and become thirstier than usual. This could be an ideal time for a litter box visit, too.

175 SCOUT OUT HOTELS

If your trip involves an overnight stay on the way, check out places beforehand since not every where accepts pets. A number of online directories list pet-friendly lodging. Many hotels and motel chains accept pets with a deposit or a nominal additional fee. Be sure you make it clear you have a kitty or two prior to check-in. You don't want a surprise visit from hotel/motel staff that could result in your cat escaping your room.

Avoid leaving your cat unattended in your room. If possible, always keep her in the carrier unless she's in your arms inside the closed room. You don't want her darting under the bed where you can't reach her. It's also a good idea to keep the "do not disturb" sign on your door at all times, whether you're inside or not.

176 FLY FEARLESSLY

If you must take your cat on a plane trip, check all your airline's requirements (as well as any governing security agency) prior to departure. You may need proof of current vaccines and there will certainly be rules about carriers, and maybe even limits on animal size. Also, it's important to investigate quarantines: some countries require as much as six months of quarantine for an animal arriving from another country!

Different airlines have varying rules about the size and structure of carriers. Check these beforehand. Generally, the carrier must be large enough that your cat can stand up and turn around in it. Soft-sided pet carriers made of nylon are sometimes allowed to exceed size limits since they are collapsible. In all cases, the carrier must have a waterproof bottom, in case of "accidents", and adequate ventilation.

177 TAKE KITTY WITH YOU

Some airlines will allow your cat to accompany you in the passenger cabin. Different airlines have different rules about flight length and the number of pets they'll allow on each flight. Your cat must remain crated throughout and the carrier will be counted as your carry-on bag or personal item. A cabin pet charge will be added to your ticket cost. It is nice to let the people sitting beside you, and in front and behind you, know you have a cat. If they are allergic, they may wish to be relocated.

At the airport, your kitty will not go through an X-ray machine, but he will need to be removed from the carrier for examination by an airline security officer.

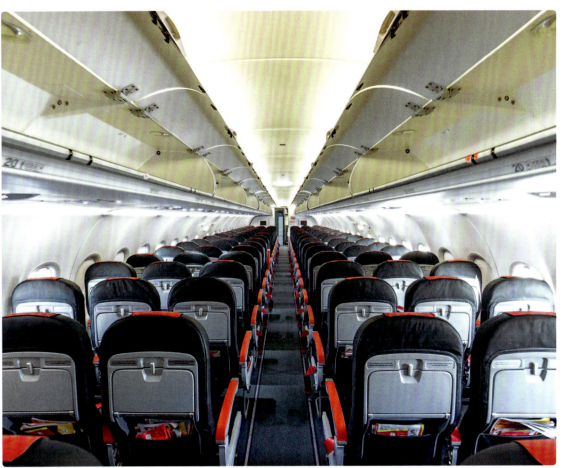

178 AVOID THE HOLD

Some airlines will only transport your cat as checked cargo. You'll pick her up as though she were baggage. We don't recommend this method of travel, as it's much riskier than having your cat in the passenger compartment. If you can't avoid your cat traveling this way, you must label her carrier "live animal" so the airline is aware that she needs to travel in a pressurized, temperature-controlled part of the airplane.

179 FIND YOUR PERFECT PET SITTER

If you're going to be traveling, hospitalized, or honeymooning, or if work or other obligations mean your cat will need a helping hand at home, you'll want to find someone you can trust to care for your darling(s). It's well worth putting in the work to find someone you trust, now and for the future, too.

The best way to find this fabulous friend of felines is by referral from your vet or someone else you know. There are also online pet-sitting registries. If you go this route, take plenty of time to really sift through the options before you choose which pros to interview. Although you may initially conduct your interviews by phone, you'll want to follow up by having any prospects come to your home to meet your pet(s) as well.

180 CHECK SITTER REFERENCES

Your sitter should provide at least three glowing references from people with pet situations similar to yours. For example, if you have a special-needs cat or a multi-pet household, make sure your prospective sitter has handled similar challenges in the past. Make sure their references are current. Take the time to contact and ask each former client for candid reviews of the pet sitter's strengths and weaknesses. As people who love their pets, they'll understand that you're worried about leaving your beloved kitty in a stranger's hands.

181 NEGOTIATE WITH THE SITTER

Always ask for important details such as the sitter's rates and insurance. Rates may be negotiable. Even if they aren't, investing in the care of your pets while you're away is worth the cost! Most pet sitters ask for fifty per cent of their fee up front. Avoid anyone who expects payment in full before your departure. If you and your kitties are thrilled with your sitter, you can always add a tip when you return (and even a souvenir from your travels!). Some pet sitters are bonded to protect their clients in the event of financial damages, but typically this is only the case if they own a licensed business or work for one. Similarly, they may have insurance for their own medical expenses, if they are injured in your home. You may not feel the need for a sitter to carry either type, but if you prefer this option, then it's good to know that some of them do—be sure to ask when you conduct your interviews. Review your homeowner's or renter's insurance for coverage in the event that your sitter is injured in your home.

FACT OR FICTION?

CATS ONLY PURR WHEN THEY'RE HAPPY
Cats do purr when they're happy, but they may also purr to soothe themselves during times of elevated stress or when they're in pain. If your kitty purrs and you suspect she's uncomfortable, observe her behavior to see if she's restless, sleepless, or unable to eat. Also, note whether the purr is fast or slow. A slow purr may indicate contentment, while a faster purr (which may be accompanied by faster and shorter breaths) can indicate distress. Some scientists think that purring releases endorphins, which are natural analgesics that may ease suffering. In other words, your kitty may self-prescribe "feel-good" medication when pain strikes.

182 GO WITH YOUR GUT

Gauge how your prospective sitter reacts to you, your family, and your pets. Be observant. Is the applicant really listening, learning, connecting, and communicating clearly and well? Are you hearing too many stories about other clients, including gossip or complaints about them? If the sitter is telling you about other clients' personal lives, understand that she might reveal your personal details to the next client.

DOES SHE LIKE YOUR PETS? Do you sense that the sitter prospect can't wait to get out the door, or is there genuine interest in every little detail about your pet family? Hopefully, the latter is true.

DOES SHE LISTEN? Are you over-explaining your cat's 10 a.m. thyroid medication routine, or going on and on about how she can't be trusted near the front door? It's OK. Pet sitters expect a little neuroticism from pet parents. If you think you're sold on this sitter, even though this is an initial interview, feel free to begin explaining your pet's routine and needs in detail. Now is the time to see if your sitter embraces the challenge or if her eyes glaze over.

WHAT ARE HER COMMITMENTS? Find out if your pet sitter will be caring for other pets during your absence (and most will). Clarify whether your cat might be exposed to other pets and in what way. Unless your kitty is from another planet, she definitely won't want your sitter bringing another cat to your home to hang out while you're away.

IS SHE TRUSTWORTHY? If your prospective sitter has a public social network page, check it out. If anything there sends up a red flag, obviously, your search for a sitter will continue—elsewhere. Spend no less than thirty minutes meeting with your sitter in your home, with your pets. In addition to providing references, your sitter should present you with valid ID and a document noting her policies and fees.

CAN SHE HANDLE YOUR CAT'S NEEDS? It's OK to ask a potential sitter about limitations. If you want to hire that delightful lady who doesn't drive, for example, make sure there's a plan in place in the event that she needs to get your huge Maine Coon—in his heavy crate—to the vet!

183 PUT YOUR CAT FIRST

As your interview goes on, you'll get an idea about whether your wannabe sitter's head is ready to explode. Maybe he has so many other clients that your situation is going to be an overload. It's not out of line to ask what other obligations he'll have while you're away. If you'll be traveling for more than a couple of days, and have asked your sitter to spend nights in your home, be sure he hasn't promised anyone else the same thing.

GET DAILY UPDATES People often fail to consider what would happen to their pet if the sitter becomes incapacitated. How would you know if your pet sitter is unconscious in hospital? And who would feed your cat? Ask your pet sitter to send you a quick daily e-mail or text update, or, if you will be out of touch, send to someone you trust. If the update doesn't come, contact your sitter and, if necessary, send someone else to feed your cats.

GET A FRIEND TO CHECK, TOO If you're going to be gone more than a few days and this is your sitter's first stay, arrange for someone you trust to check in on the cats at least once a week. Let the sitter know that this will happen. Having regular reports from someone who knows your kitties will put your mind at rest. It will also reassure your sitter that should any problems arise, there will be someone at hand to help. In the unlikely event that the sitter is not as committed as you expected, your friend can alert you to that, too.

184 REVIEW THE BACKUP PLAN

Your sitter should have a backup sitter on deck in the event that she can't complete the job. Find out if this is the case. Make sure to get that person's name and contact information, and check their references, too.

To cover all bases . . . you should also have someone in mind—maybe your friend (*see* item 183)—who can also help out if the sitter and her understudy can't be there for your kitty!

185 DO YOUR PAPERWORK!

Many pet sitters and agencies have forms where you'll note your contact information while traveling, as well as the names of people who should be contacted if you are unreachable. This may include people with keys to your home in case your sitter gets locked out. (It can happen!) If a form isn't presented to you, create your own.

Write out an instruction list that explains in detail what you expect. You may want to leave a copy in your own home and give your sitter one as well. Include the following:

VITAL INFORMATION

- An outline of your pet and house rules, include as much information as you can.
- Details of health issues or medications and your kitty's likes and dislikes. Make a kitty biography complete with photo.
- Your vet's name, address, and contact infomation, and the location and number of the nearest pet emergency hospital. Put your pet's medical records and microchip details someplace handy for your sitter to refer to at any time during your absence.
- A note of where keys will be left, if you didn't give them out during the interview, codes needed to access your home, and any other security requirements.
- The names and contact details of anyone your sitter may need to get in touch with in your absence, such as your landlord.
- Leaving instructions on how to work your complicated TV system and its three different remotes would be a nice touch!

ON THE CATWALK

NYAN CAT

Probably the most noteworthy thing about Nyan Cat is that he is not a real cat, nor has he ever been. A GIF animation consisting of a cat's smiley face with a Pop-Tart body trailing a rainbow, Nyan is the brainchild of Christopher Torres from Dallas, Texas. Torres initally designed the cat GIF to raise money for the Red Cross. He called his GIF Pop-Tart Cat. However, Nyan took off in an unexpected way.

BIRTH NAME
Pop-Tart Cat

STAGE NAME
Nyan Cat

BORN
April 2, 2011, in Dallas, Texas

YOUTUBE HITS
150 million plus

TRIVIA
There are Nyan ringtones, apps, games, songs, and a cryptocurrency called Nyancoin.

A song called *Nyanyanyanyanyanyanya*, which means "meow" in Japanese, had been placed on a Japanese video site in 2010. A YouTube user called Sara linked a cover version of this song with the GIF, just three days after Torres uploaded it.

The name of the song has become inextricably linked with the GIF, which is now known to millions of people as Nyan Cat. The original Nyan Cat video features Nyan Cat flying through a starlit sky "singing" *Nyanyanyanyanyanyanya*. It has the distinction of being the most watched "cat" video on YouTube, with over 131 million views. There are numerous other videos, including *Nyan Cat Falls in Love* with 2.9 million views and *Nyans around the World* with nearly 6.2 million views.

Nyan Cat has a website, nyan.cat, which is operated by Torres.

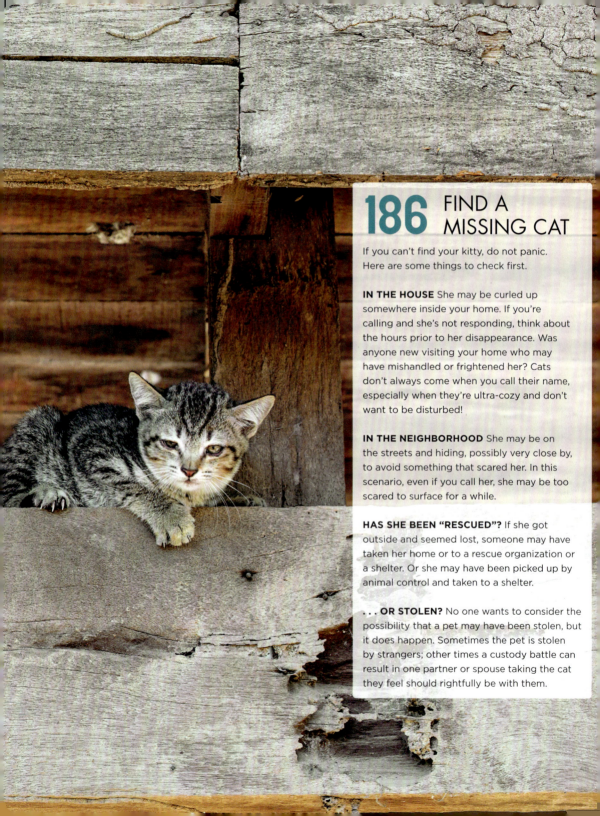

186 FIND A MISSING CAT

If you can't find your kitty, do not panic. Here are some things to check first.

IN THE HOUSE She may be curled up somewhere inside your home. If you're calling and she's not responding, think about the hours prior to her disappearance. Was anyone new visiting your home who may have mishandled or frightened her? Cats don't always come when you call their name, especially when they're ultra-cozy and don't want to be disturbed!

IN THE NEIGHBORHOOD She may be on the streets and hiding, possibly very close by, to avoid something that scared her. In this scenario, even if you call her, she may be too scared to surface for a while.

HAS SHE BEEN "RESCUED"? If she got outside and seemed lost, someone may have taken her home or to a rescue organization or a shelter. Or she may have been picked up by animal control and taken to a shelter.

. . . OR STOLEN? No one wants to consider the possibility that a pet may have been stolen, but it does happen. Sometimes the pet is stolen by strangers; other times a custody battle can result in one partner or spouse taking the cat they feel should rightfully be with them.

187 START A SEARCH

If you've lost a cat, make sure that you safely contain any other pets in your home before you begin looking for your missing cat. First thoroughly search inside your house. When you go out searching, leave a door to the outside slightly open, if possible, so your kitty can come in should he return of his own accord.

The first place to check outside is the area closest to your home, including under the building. An obvious hiding place is a crawlspace, but you'll also want to look for other openings, even those that seem too small for your cat to go through. A scared animal can contort himself to fit into places he might otherwise avoid.

If you spy your cat in a bush or in a hidey hole, try to lure him out using comforting words that he is used to. Try not to project your concern. If he doesn't come to you, place a favorite treat a few inches away from you, urging him to take the treat so you can pluck him up. If this doesn't work, and you can't stay with him until it does, you may want to leave a trail of treats—one every two feet or so—leading back to the door or window you've left open for his safe passage back indoors. Otherwise, you may wish to set a humane trap (*see* item 195). Be sure it's out of the sight of strangers, tended by someone you trust, if you can't be there.

It may sound obvious, but it's important to get the word out ASAP that your kitty is missing. A kitty on the loose may be scared, and could randomly run in a direction that takes him away from home, and he might not know how to find his way back. Don't assume he'll return on his own any time soon.

LOST CAT

Name: Jasper, also responds to "Jaspy"

Description: Brown and black striped cat with long hair and green eyes.

Last seen: Green Street on Oct. 5 around 7pm (he ran out my door)

REWARD!!! 555-0123

Kitty 555-0123 (repeated on tear-off tabs)

188 CREATE A FLYER

Post "Lost Cat" flyers featuring a clear, current picture of your kitty around your neighborhood, making enough copies to put one on every neighbor's doorstep, and/or on their car windshields. Post them everywhere, including at the vet's, the supermarket, and animal rescue centers. Keep it simple. Use the example here:

- Put LOST CAT at the top in large, easy-to-read, bold letters.
- Add a brief description: "Brown and black striped cat with long hair and green eyes." Don't assume that people will know your cat's particular breed.
- Give his name: this makes it easier for someone to lure him.
- Include the date, time, and location he went missing.
- Mention a reward, if you want to give one (don't say an amount).
- Don't forget your telephone number—in large numbers.

It is worth keeping back one distinguishing characteristic your kitty has, such as a kinked tail or an extralarge spot on one side. If someone calls claiming to have found her, you can ask them to describe this unique feature, which will prove whether they've seen her or have her. (Of course, a cell phone photo or video can prove this, too.) Be sure your cat is returned to you before you actually give out any reward you've offered!

189 CALL, SEARCH, FEED, AND WAIT

Obviously, you also need to get out and call your kitty by name. Enlist family and friends to canvass your neighborhood in all directions. Don't try to predict where your cat may have gone. The best times to look for him are in the evening and around dawn.

SEARCH THE NEIGHBORHOOD Walk or drive through your neighborhood several times a day. Ask neighbors, postal carriers, and delivery people if they've seen your cat. Have your flyer to hand (*see* opposite) or give out a recent photograph of him, and information on how you can be reached if he's found.

SET UP FEEDING STATIONS Put a feeding spot just outside your home with food and water. Change it regularly to keep it attractive to a cat. Ask your neighbors if they'll do the same for you. Naturally, you'll have better luck with this if you give them with necessary supplies. Remember to ask them not just to feed your cat, but to alert you the minute he shows up munching!

BE PREPARED TO WAIT The friendliest pet may quickly become terrified and act like he's wild. When lost, he may hide or run away from people—even you. If you see him, don't chase after him, sit on the ground, and speak in a comforting, relaxed tone, frequently repeating his name and familiar phrases. It could take a long time—hours—but it may comfort him enough to stay put and eventually come to you. Bring treats and offer him those to help remind him who loves him.

190 LEAVE NO STONE UNTURNED

Look, look, and look again. You want kitty back safely at home, so stop at nothing. Here are a few more ideas that you might want to try:

HIRE A PET DETECTIVE If you can afford to do so, consider hiring a pet detective to continue searching and following up with neighbors, shelters, vets, and rescue groups. Choose a seasoned detective with valid, recent references. He should have working relationships with local rescue organizations and city shelters.

Detectives usually charge a flat daily fee, along with any expenses they incur. Thoroughly check the references of a prospective pet detective. Find out his or her rate of success and how long it has taken in the past to locate lost pets.

JOIN LOST-AND-FOUND NETWORKING SERVICES There are many online pet networking operations. Some are free registries where both lost and found animals are posted. These are updated frequently. You can find many of them with a quick internet search. Another good resource for networking assistance is a national or international rescue organization, where referrals to other registries will likely be available.

For a fee, some services will contact hundreds of households in your area with an automated phone call that includes the details about your missing pet, along with your contact information. Fees for this type of service vary, depending on the number of calls you'd like made on your behalf, but they are well worth considering. Success stories abound for networking services. They make it as easy as possible for those who have lost pets to find them, and for those who have found lost pets and want to help worried pet parents.

CHECK SOCIAL MEDIA Numerous Facebook, Twitter, and other social media channels exist, free of charge, for the posting of lost and found animals. They inspire communities to keep a constant eye out for missing pets, and they have a high success rate.

You should also post directly to your own Facebook page, too, and ask your friends to share your post with all their friends.

FOLLOW UP LEADS As much as possible, keep public any communication you have with someone who claims to have your pet. If you plan to meet the person, do it in a public place. If you are meeting alone, let other people know when and where you're going and post those details on the social media page. Ask for a video or photo transmission of your kitty in real time via cell phone.

191 GIVE KITTY AN OPENING

Leave a door or window slightly open for your cat to use if she returns on her own (only if this is safe for you and your family!). Naturally, you need to keep other indoor pets in a safe place away from the open door or window to prevent them from getting out as well. Sometimes a frightened pet may not respond to being called, but will sneak back home once things settle down and have gone quiet, particularly at night.

192 GET THE WORD OUT

The more people who know your cat is lost, the more the word will spread. Knock on doors to ask if anyone has seen your kitty. Have extra flyers with you to again hand out—even if you've already left flyers at all the same homes. If someone you ask has a garage, see if you can check for him there yourself.

193 USE ALL YOUR RESOURCES

Here are some more ideas for what to do should your kitty go for a wander.

CHECK LOCAL GROUPS AND ORGANIZATIONS

• Right away, call and visit animal shelters, since it can take a while for a shelter to post animals they take in on their website. (Find local shelters online or in the phone book.)

• Register your cat as missing with as many shelters as possible, giving them a description and photographs.

• Check all shelters' online registries several times a day and visit daily, if possible.

• During shelter visits, check all areas, including the infirmary. Ask if any deceased cats were brought in.

• Contact all local animal rescue groups to see if a well-meaning person found your kitty and brought her in. If

the group has a lot of cats, yours may not have been noticed, so visit and follow up. If they have volunteers who foster displaced kitties, someone may already be caring for your kitty.

• Contact your local and state police departments, especially if you believe your pet was stolen. Your city council member may also be of help.

• Call veterinary clinics, including emergency veterinary hospitals, both inside and outside your local area.

• Call all city animal services, the highway department, grooming shops, and pet stores—basically, call any place where someone who finds a lost cat may take her.

194 PLACE AN AD, WITH CARE

While it's not a bad idea to place a "lost pet" ad in your local paper's classified section, do so with caution. There are unscrupulous people intent on extorting money from emotionally vulnerable strangers, so don't give too much information about your cat, and don't offer too generous a reward. In describing her, include her sex, age, weight, breed, and color. But leave out one identifying characteristic, and if someone claims to have found her, ask that person to describe this for you, or better yet, send you a video or photo of the kitty via cell phone.

Be wary if someone says they've found your cat and asks for money. Ask them to describe the pet thoroughly before you offer any more information or arrange to pick up your cat. Have the person call your cell and use an app such as Facetime, Skype, or Google Hangouts so you can see your cat in real time. If this isn't possible, get the person to text you a photo of your cat.

195 SET A HUMANE TRAP

You should be able to rent or borrow a humane trap from an animal shelter or cat rescue group. Traps are safe and simple to use. A representative from the organization can explain how they work.

Do not leave the loaded trap unattended. Only put food in it and load it when you can directly monitor it. You'll need a small amount of very appetizing food that's fragrant (to a cat, at least). Canned tuna and chicken nuggets are good. Try whenever you can—people often have the most luck after dark.

Set the trap out of sight of strangers, close to your home and as near as possible to where your cat went missing.

Once you catch your darling, don't open the trap until she's safely, securely inside—preferably isolated in a room where she can spend a little time secluded, with fresh food and water, litter, and nonstop snuggles.

196 DON'T GIVE UP!

Naturally, your kitty has a better chance of being returned sooner if he always wears a collar and an ID tag with your name, address, and telephone number. But no matter what, keep in mind that cats are tenacious, and can hole up somewhere for incredibly long periods of time.

Your kitty is a family member, and you wouldn't give up looking for a lost family member, so keep an active search going for at least two to three months. Lost cats have been returned to their homes weeks, months, and sometimes even years, later!

You'd be surprised how many people will help you look and lend support in any way they can. As a courtesy, once your kitty is returned, give everyone who knew he was missing the good news. They'll be thrilled and relieved!

197 APPROACH AN INJURED CAT

Caring for a cat who is in physical distress means proceeding with extreme caution. Don't pick up an injured cat right away; rather, speak to her in soothing tones as you approach her slowly. Then, work your way down to her level until you are crouching next to her on the ground. Reach out very slowly and gently, without sudden movements. If she lets you, begin to stroke her, steering clear—at least at first—of the injured area. Injured cats will likely feel insecure or even threatened, which means they may dart away from you (risking further injury), or even scratch and claw at you. If you need to pick the cat up, do so slowly and gently, without any jarring motions. If you have a towel or a blanket, wrap the kitty up, both to make her feel secure and so that you avoid injury from her panicky claws. Gloves can be very helpful as well.

198 GROOM FOR HEALTH

Beyond keeping fur balls at bay (see below), regularly brushing your cat has many advantages. It helps to distribute natural oils on the surface of her coat, clears away irritants and—believe it or not—can be a nice bonding exercise for you and kitty.

To brush your cat, use a bevy of brushes. First, use a comb to untangle knots and make kitty look pretty.

Then gently brush over her fur with a wire brush to collect loose hairs. Finally, use an old toothbrush to carefully groom the fur on and around her oh-so-pretty face. You can even buy gloves with brushlike bristles on them, so that a brushing session can feel just like a wonderful all-over petting. Make sure you go over all of her fur, including the tail and the ears.

WHAT ARE FUR BALLS?

Fur balls form when your cat grooms. As he licks himself, small structures on his tongue hook onto dead hairs on his body and pull them out. He then swallows them. Most hairs pass through his body without issue, but some get stuck in the digestive system and he will vomit them up in the form of fur balls (which, when eliminated, look more like tubes). The more meticulous your kitty is, the more likely he'll suffer from fur balls.

199 COIF YOUR CAT

Giving your cat a haircut? These days, lots of cute (or even dramatic) "styles" are offered at your local cat groomer or, if you're attempting to groom kitty's coat yourself, an internet search will give you plenty of ideas.

Certain grooming styles can help your cat (and may amuse you, to boot). For instance, shaving the belly of a very hairy cat is a mat remedy. For older cats, long-haired cats, and any cats who struggle to wash themselves after a trip to the litter box, a hygiene cut (in which fur around the anus is removed) helps to keep the area clean and to prevent mats and discomfort.

Certain cat salons offer something called a lion cut, where they cut most of the fur very short (or shave it altogether), leaving a furry face and neck plus tufts on the tail and feet. Regardless of whether you find the lion cut funny or glamorous, your cat will find it keeps her cool and helps her avoid matting, which is especially welcome for long-haired kitties in the height of summer.

200 BATHE OR NOT?

When it comes to cats, baths are optional. You see, kitties spend a huge portion of their day washing themselves. So unless they've fallen in the mud or gotten drenched in maple syrup after leaping onto the table, they don't really need our help.

Unsurprisingly, our feline friends aren't fans of being soaked with water and then poked and prodded. But if your cat needs something washed off her coat pronto and you think she can handle a bath, it's worth putting in the effort to make the process enjoyable for you both. First off, it's important to keep baths short and sweet— just three to five minutes should be fine. Test the water temperature to make sure kitty will be comfortable. Also, tune into her body language. If she's feeling stressed, don't force a long, drawn-out bath session. And take a minute to consider how you're feeling, too; if you're impatient after a hard day, wait until you're more relaxed, as your ultra-intuitive cat will likely pick up on that mood.

201

WORK THOSE CLAWS

Face it: your cat will scratch. It's a natural instinct and necessary for claw health. You can't stop kitty from using those sharp little needles, but you can control where he scratches by setting up scratch zones in your home. Before you create a scratch zone for your kitty-cat, consider the following:

HEIGHT Have at least two scratching posts that are tall enough to encourage your cat to stretch right up to reach the top of them. They should measure at least three feet (1 m) tall.

TEXTURE Most pet stores sell ready-made scratching devices such as bark-covered "logs" or cardboard scratching boxes that lie on the floor. You can add extra texture to your scratching places, too. For instance, wind sisal rope around parts of the posts, giving your cat a place to grab onto.

POSITION Place one scratching post in the place your cat tends to scratch most often—by the couch, maybe—and another in the area where he sleeps. Cats like to stretch when they wake up and this is often followed by a nice, long scratch. Ahhh. Set up other small scratching boxes throughout the house. They tend to wear out quickly, so be sure to replace them regularly. Add hanging strings, balls, or wire toys to make each scratch-here spot ultra-attractive to your scratch-happy kitty.

202 GIVE A PAW-DICURE

Cats can be tetchy about having their nails clipped, so begin slowly and with care. If possible, start trimming your indoor cat's nails at a young age so she gets used to it. If you adopt an adult cat, or are clipping your adult cat's nails for the first time, introduce her to it gradually.

MAKE A START For several days in a row, hold your cat on your lap as if you're going to clip her nails (A), but gently massage her paws instead. Then, on a day when she seems relaxed, hold a paw in your hand and press lightly on the bottom of it, pushing out the claw (B). Use a finger on one side of a toe, and another on the bottom (toe pad). Gently squeeze each toe to extend each claw. Repeat this a few times over a few days if necessary.

GO FOR A CLIP Once the kitty is relaxed with the massage, repeat it, but then use a pair of sharp claw trimmers (or human nail clippers) to remove only the tip (hook) of the claw (C). Be careful not to damage the

vein that runs through the quick—the pink part near the paw (D), before the nail curves. Cutting any part of this is super-painful. If your cat balks at a full manicure, ease her into the idea by clipping just one or two nails in each session at first. Never rush; never force it.

REPEAT THE REWARDS Even though your cat may not love it, nail-clipping has its advantages: greatly reducing damage to furniture! Regular trimming—about every other week—will make the quick recede so that you can trim the nails shorter, further reducing that pesky damage.

OUTDOOR CATS

Skip manicure sessions on outdoor cats. Consider only lightly trimming the front nails of your outdoor kitty, and definitely leave those back nails intact so your cat can climb trees, and even fend off attackers, unfettered.

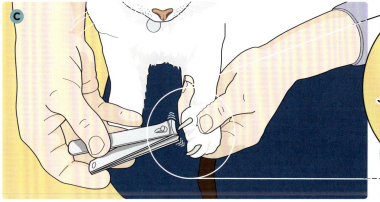

cut here   quick

203 WEATHERPROOF YOUR FURRY FRIEND

Face it: your feline is a wimp about weather. Most kitties hate getting snowed or rained on—oh, the indignity!—even if they like to spend time outdoors. When it's very cold, try to keep your outdoor cat inside with you, as he's vulnerable to frostbite. Windchill and sudden dips in temperature can wreak havoc on exposed skin, like your cat's nose. During cold months, offer your cat a tad more food and water than usual, as the biological processes required to stay warm will deplete his energy.

Being too hot is no picnic either; in the summer, encourage your cat to drink plenty of water, even if it has to be from his favorite water fountain: the tap (*see* item 166). Consider giving him a haircut (*see* item 199).

204 PROVIDE KITTY PERCHES

We know how much cats love to perch on high objects and look down on us. If you really want to spoil your feline friend, try crafting a tailor-made perch to rival the back of the sofa and the tall bookcase, where she already spends hours and hours. You can find plenty of options online, from cat trees to elaborate multilevel structures made from sanded wood. Many of these ideas require power tools, a few hours, and a number of dollars—all well and good if you enjoy DIY. But the bottom line is that your cat won't be impressed by fancy craftsmanship; she'll be grateful if you just, say, arrange a sturdy piece of furniture or another object that will make a safe and cozy hangout beside one or more windows—through which she can look longingly at moving objects (any will do).

205 CONSIDER A CATERRARIUM

A caterarium is an enclosed natural area where your cat can safely venture "outside" without being able to leave your property where she risks getting into trouble. While a "catio" is an enclosed patio, a caterarium is usually a bit of your back or side yard, ideally with a floor of grass or astroturf, and with sides and roof of wire or plastic fencing so that your cat can see out, but can't get out. You can build it adjacent to your house, and place a cat door in a window screen to allow your cat easy access. Be sure you include a secure gate that you can use for access if necessary. Your cat will love it if you add shelves to hang out on and shady spots to lie in!

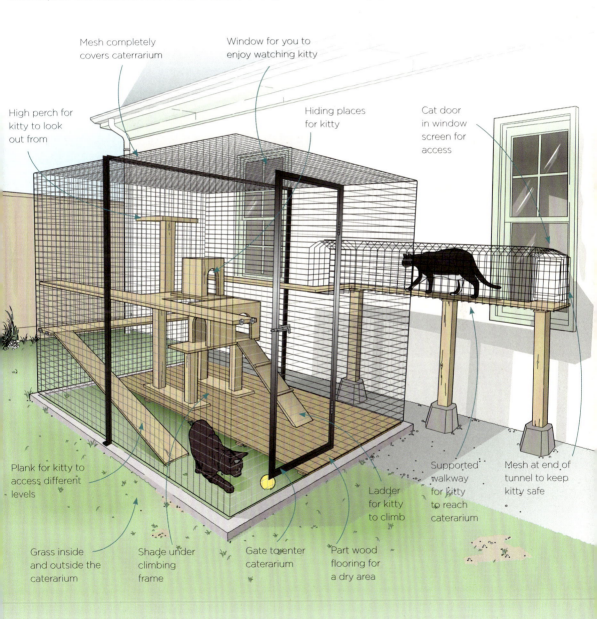

Mesh completely covers caterarium

Window for you to enjoy watching kitty

High perch for kitty to look out from

Hiding places for kitty

Cat door in window screen for access

Plank for kitty to access different levels

Supported walkway for kitty to reach caterarium

Mesh at end of tunnel to keep kitty safe

Ladder for kitty to climb

Grass inside and outside the caterarium

Shade under climbing frame

Gate to enter caterarium

Part wood flooring for a dry area

206 BRUSH THOSE GNASHERS

To minimize plaque, control tartar, avoid dangerous infections, and prevent the need for expensive veterinary procedures, regular brushing is key.

WHAT YOU NEED Buy a toothbrush tailor-made for kitties—your own old toothbrush will be too rough— and some kitty toothpaste. This comes in appetizing flavors like poultry, beef, and seafood.

HOW TO BRUSH As with nail clipping (*see* item 202), gradually introduce toothbrushing. Over a period of several weeks, expose your cat to toothpaste by first letting him lick it off your finger, then putting it on a feline toothbrush and again letting him lick it off. At some point, try brushing his teeth with your finger. Soon he'll be comfortable enough to let you put the toothbrush in his mouth and gently brush.

207 SAY AHH!

Sometimes, even a toothbrushing a day can't keep the dentist away. When tooth and gum diseases strike unlucky kitties, dental procedures such as extractions or a scale and polish are sometimes necessary. These are usually carried out under anesthesia.

THE BEFORE Your veterinarian may have a to-do (or don't-do) list for you and kitty to follow in preparation for the procedure. Different dental conditions require different prep work; be sure to ask your vet when your cat can (and cannot) eat or drink, which pills he should be taking, and about anything else you can do to make the big day go as smoothly as possible.

AND THE AFTER When the procedure's over—yay!—and your feline friend is recovering at home, safe and sound, reintroduce food slowly. Usually, the vet will tell you how long to wait before feeding and will recommend giving small portions every few hours for about a day before returning to the normal routine.

208 FOLLOW ANOTHER DENTAL ROUTINE

Some cats detest having their teeth brushed, no matter how sensitively you introduce the idea. If this sounds like your kitty, don't give up—just continue to take it slowly! In the meantime, consider other approaches. Oral rinses and gels, medicated sprays, good-for-teeth treats, and store-bought "dental toys" can fight plaque and tartar, too. Certain cat food is formulated to keep teeth healthy; ask your vet for advice. If your cat's teeth are generally healthy, spending time and energy on them may not seem like a top priority, but trust us: as he gets older, which is when teeth problems often show up, you'll be glad you invested in a great in-home dental routine from day one.

209 LAUNDER THOSE LUGS

It should not be necessary to clean your cat's ears unless there's a chance she's got mites or if she's prone to ear infections. However, if your vet says they need cleaning, here's how you should do it. Many ear-cleaning solutions exist; to be on the safe side, choose one that is designed for sensitive skin. Douse a cotton swab or tissue with the solution. Gently fold back the tip of her ear, and with a very light touch, clean the inside of the ear, being careful not to go too deep into the ear canal.

210 LET MUSIC SOOTHE THE BEAST

Some people find that music soothes their anxious kitties and helps with nervous behaviors like compulsive furniture scratching or even territorial spraying. You may need to experiment with different styles of music and volume levels to find your cat's perfect groove. Some experts claim that cats, like many humans, find classical music especially relaxing. Some innovative musicians produce special music meant for cats to enjoy, and these compositions can be found by searching online. You may discover, though, that any type of music calms your kitty; if you're lucky, she'll curl up and cuddle with you as your favorite tunes play.

211 WATCH KITTY WATCHING TV

Some parents frown on letting their kids zone out for hours in front of the boob tube. Luckily, as cat parents we can be a little more lax—as long as kitty's not batting at your expensive new flatscreen, claws outstretched. Why do cats go goggle-eyed when the TV is switched on? As with so much funny feline behavior, the reason is likely tied to your cat's deeply ingrained animal instincts. In other words, when he sees little objects moving around on the screen, your cat's little brain says "hunt." And so he stares, transfixed by his prey, calculating how to pounce on it. That's one theory, anyway; it's possible he just likes cable.

212 PUT YOUR KNOWLEDGE TO THE TEST

As well as playing a key role in popular media, cats are part of our heritage. These small furry creatures have managed to get into every corner of our lives, including films and literature. Most cat owners would argue that their cat is highly intelligent, and of course, they are right, but are cats brighter than dogs? Well, that's a question that's very difficult to answer, although you could sidestep it by saying cats are clever at being cats, and dogs at being dogs. Here are a few other brainteasers to keep you on your toes.

1 PUT THESE AMERICAN WILDCATS IN ORDER OF HEIGHT.

☐ Jaguar

☐ Lynx

☐ Cougar

2 WHERE IS IT BELIEVED THAT CATS FIRST BECAME DOMESTICATED?

☐ United Kingdom

☐ China

☐ Egypt

3 WHAT DISTINGUISHED ERNEST HEMINGWAY'S CATS?

☐ They had no tails.

☐ They were tabbies.

☐ They were polydactyl (extra toes).

4 WHAT WAS THE NAME OF THE CAT IN BREAKFAST AT TIFFANY'S?

☐ Puss

☐ Cat

☐ Ginger

5 WHICH HAS THE HEAVIEST BRAIN RELATIVE TO BODY SIZE?

☐ Dog

☐ Cat

☐ Horse

6 WHAT BREED OF CAT APPEARS IN THE CLASSIC CARTOON FILM LADY AND THE TRAMP?

☐ Siamese

☐ Persian

☐ Abyssinian

ANSWERS

1 Lynx 22 inches (56 cm); jaguar 30 inches (76 cm); cougar 35 inches (89 cm). **2** Egypt around 4,000 years ago, although new evidence suggests it might have been much earlier. **3** They were polydactyl. **4** The answer is Cat. The cat actor was called Orangey. **5** Dog. But it's close: a dog's brain is 1.2 percent while a cat's is 1 percent. Horses lag behind at 0.25 percent. **6** There were two Siamese cats and they were very wicked.

213 PURRFECT YOUR PORTRAITS

You and your family love your cat and all her funny antics and you'll want to share the love (and show her off, of course). The most popular way to do this is via YouTube, although sharing on Instagram, Facebook, and Twitter are all surefire ways to get friends—and many other people—admiring your clever kitty.

1 CARRY YOUR CAMERA Take your cell phone with you as you move around the house, you never know when you'll come across your cat in a perfect pose.

2 TAKE SNEAK SHOTS Rather than have your kitty posing, all self aware—although this can be good, too—take pics of her doing her thing: stretching, rolling, patting a ball, stalking a leaf. You get the idea.

3 GET DOWN It's often a lot of fun and more effective to take photographs from a cat's-eye view of the world, so try crouching down at her level, or even lower, before getting snap happy.

4 KEEP IT SIMPLE Remember cameras lenses are not as sophisticated as human eyes. You'll get better results in a good light and with a plain background, such as a light carpet or wood floor.

5 BE FUSSY It is worth spending some time going through the results of your photo shoot and deleting anything that is less than perfect. Pick just a few special pictures to share with the world.

6 TRY EFFECTS Once you've got a few shots, have a go at editing. Aside from cropping in, which can transform a photo, there is endless fun to be had playing around with the special effects available on cell phones, or why not download an app?

7 PRINT YOUR HANDIWORK Good photos deserve to be seen and make great room decorations when blown up or put in a pretty frame, or you can have a T-shirt printed with your pusscat on the front.

214 CARE FOR YOUR OLD-TIMER

Without a doubt, the hardest part about having a pet is when they are growing old and their health is failing, and it comes the moment to say goodbye. The time leading up to this sad event is very special. It's when the balance changes from your cat not needing much from you, to her needing you to be there more often to keep her as comfortable as possible. This may include giving medications and making some alterations in your home such as adding steps to places she can no longer reach by jumping up or down. Look out for other signs that your cat needs help:

- She may not groom as often, so her hair doesn't feel clean like it used to. Be ready to brush her.

- Cats often don't show when they're in pain. Pay close attention to her so you know what she is likely experiencing (*see* item 139). Try to make each day special and give her lots of love.
- Older cats lose body fat, so they feel the cold more. Consider buying a special cat heating pad. These provide a very small amount of heat—perfect for a cat to lie on at night (normal heating pads get far too hot for this purpose; do not use them).

Remember, an old cat is like an old person—with all the various aches and pains and medical issues that arise. This is your chance to pay your beloved cat back for all the love she has shown you throughout the years.

215 FACE END-OF-LIFE CARE

When your cat is old and has medical issues, you may have to make some hard decisions about whether to continue with treatments that are designed to solve or slow the progress of medical problems, or whether to switch to palliative care, which is just intended to keep your cat comfortable for the rest of his life. A surgery to remove a tumor, for example, may be appropriate to save the life of a younger cat, but may be too much for an older cat to endure. Work with your vet to decide what treatments have a chance of prolonging your cat's life, and whether that remaining life will have good quality. It is too easy for us to focus only on keeping our beloved feline friend alive and with us, not seeing that his life is so compromised that the more humane thing to do is to say goodbye, even though this is so hard for us. Your vet has been through this many times, and you may have friends who have also had old pets, so let them share their insights—they may see things you cannot see.

216 GIVE THE GREATEST GIFT

The sad truth is that we all are going to pass away, and this is, of course, true for your cat. No amount of care or effort you put out will change this. The question is not if you will need to say goodbye, but when. We have the opportunity, if we choose to use it, to put a stop to suffering and ask a vet to calmly and painlessly end the life of our beloved friend. Some vets will come to your home to do this, which may make things easier.

TAKE COMFORT This is one of the hardest decisions you will have to make. You may fear saying goodbye too soon, and perhaps denying a loving cat a few days more of life, or you may fear saying goodbye too late, allowing her to suffer needlessly. Often, if your elderly or ill cat stops eating for several days and there is no medically curable cause, it is a sign she is ready to go.

LISTEN TO YOUR HEART Remember, there are no right or wrong answers. Consult with your family and your vet, and make the best decision you can when the moment comes. Be comforted that letting go of your cat is really preventing suffering. It may help to remember that even a few extra days at the end of life will likely not be comfortable days for your cat. Saying goodbye to her and helping her avoid needless pain is the last and greatest gift you can give her.

217 MEMORIALIZE YOUR FRIEND

You bonded closely with your cat, but he's no longer there when you wake up or when you get home from work. Whenever you think about him, you have to hold back tears. When you're alone, the tears flow. You can't erase this pain—nor would you want to. Only time and warm memories will bring you comfort. But you can begin to feel better by paying tribute to your cat's unique life and special personality. A thoughtful commemoration can give meaning to his memory and will eventually allow you to move forward with an open heart.

CONSIDER A CREATIVE OUTLET Write a story, essay, or poem, or simply keep a diary of your feelings, whether you put it in a drawer to re-read during hard times or share it with the people in your life. A photo montage or video album are other great memorials.

SHARE YOUR FEELINGS Sharing your sadness on social media will bring many comforting comments and let you know you're not alone. Many people have been through this type of pain when they have lost a beloved pet and they will know exactly how you are suffering. More and more, people are holding funerals to pay tribute to the pets they loved. Think about gathering loved ones together to share stories and memories about your wonderful, silly, at times crazy cat.

MAKE A DIFFERENCE Be sure to tell your friends and loved ones of your loss. Consider asking them to donate to a local cat rescue organization in memory of your cat. This could help many other kitties in need. Eventually, even though you'll still miss your beloved friend, you'll smile when you look back on the happy times you shared.

218 MEND YOUR BROKEN HEART

After saying goodbye to your beloved pet, you will likely need some time to grieve. Some people find comfort in bringing a new cat into their home right away, and others need to wait a while. There is no right or wrong. A catless home can feel strange when you're used to having purry paws in it. When you're ready to start considering opening your home to a new cat in need, visit Adopt-a-Pet.com or Petfinder.com and contact your local shelter or rescue. There is no way to replace your wonderful cat whose memory you will cherish forever, but you can provide a home for another cat that deserves a home and is in need of love too. You will know when the time is right and that will be the lucky day for your next new friend.

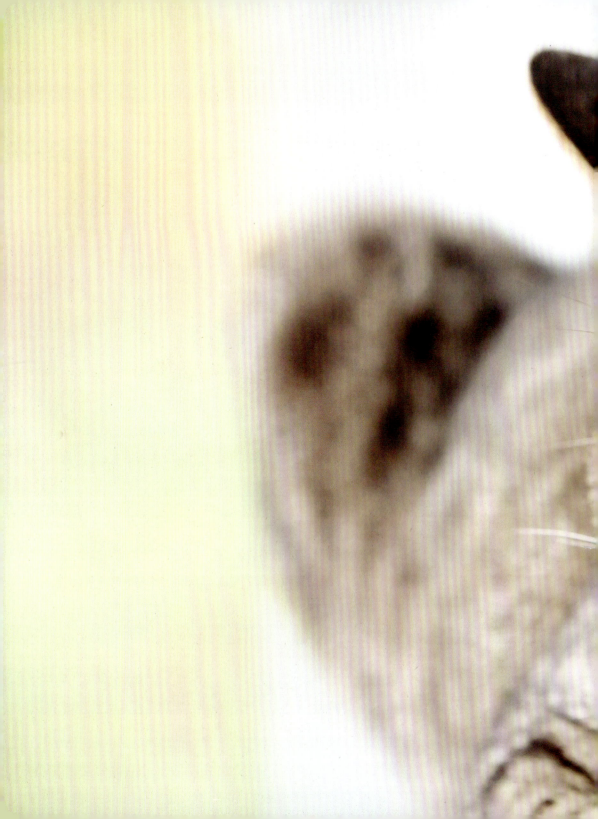

INDEX

Numbers refer to the item number. Unnumbered items are indexed by the numbered item that they follow. For example, *"following* 84" means that you can find this information in the box that appears after the text numbered 84.

CREDITS

WELDON**OWEN**

PRESIDENT & PUBLISHER Roger Shaw
ASSOCIATE PUBLISHER Mariah Bear
EDITORS Bridget Fitzerald, Ian Cannon
CREATIVE DIRECTOR Kelly Booth
ART DIRECTOR Allister Fein
ILLUSTRATION COORDINATOR Conor Buckley
IMAGING MANAGER Don Hill

MOSELEY ROAD INC

PRESIDENT Sean Moore
PRODUCTION DIRECTOR Adam Moore
EDITOR Jo Weeks
ILLUSTRATORS Andy Crisp and Liberum Donum
DESIGN Philippa Baile
Special thanks to Dan Connolly for indexing services, Jo Walton for compiling the credits, and for photographing the pill pockets, and Tamara White for photo retouching.

Adopt-a-Pet.com

PRESIDENT David Meyer
EXECUTIVE DIRECTOR Abbie Moore
SPOKESPERSON Dr. Pia Salk

Special thanks to Jennifer Warner Jacobsen, Nancy Van Iderstine, and Erica Gordon-Mallin for their contributions to this book.

ABOUT OUR SPONSORS:

Purina has been a leader in pet care and nutrition for 90 years and makes some of the most popular and trusted pet care brands, spanning dog and cat food, snacks and litter. Guided by the belief that pets and people are better together, Purina partners with animal welfare organizations across the U.S. to nourish shelter pets and support programs that enrich the lives of pets and the people who love them.

Petco Foundation. Since 1999, the Petco Foundation has invested more than $167 million in lifesaving animal welfare work across the country. In partnership with local animal welfare organizations and Petco stores, the Petco Foundation has helped more than five million pets find loving families by encouraging communities to Think Adoption First. Visit petcofoundation.org to learn more about how you can get involved.

Science For A Better Life

Bayer Animal Health. Bayer produces flea, tick, and heartworm preventatives, including Advantage Multi® for Cats (imidacloprid+moxidectin), Advantage Multi® for Dogs (imidacloprid+moxidectin), K9 Advantix® II for dogs, Seresto® for dogs or cats, and Advantage® II for cats. Bayer's Friends in Need program provides Bayer flea and tick products at discounted rates to animal shelters and welfare organizations.